My Tears Have

A Story!

By

Darlene Williams

Dedication

I DEDICATE THIS BOOK TO EVERYONE WHO MAY HAVE GONE THRU SO MUCH TRAUMA THAT THEY FEEL ALL HOPE IS GONE... JUST KNOW JOY COMES IN THE MORNING! (Psalm 30:5)

Acknowledgements

To God, who has and is still showing me how to love him as a Father! I could not have done this without Him at all. He was there when no one else was there. He loved me when I did not even love myself.

To my children – Kiwaun, Kierra, Karlief, Keshane, and Kayla, and my grandbabies – Nariah, Keyon, Musa, and Kimora. I love you all a lot! It's because of you I can strive towards being a great mom and glam-ma. I love each of you dearly and want you to know you are kings and queens destined to change the world!

To Pastor and Sister Brown. Even though I'm not with your ministry anymore, I'll never forget the foundation you both implanted in me. I appreciate the kindness you showed to my boys. And, when I was in need, Sister Brown was always there, no matter what. I'll never forget that!

To Apostle Kevin and Elect Lady Deirdre Cunningham. Thanks for helping me when I was broken, felt lifeless, hated myself, was on the verge of losing my mind, suicidal and in abusive relationships. you helped me build my confidence again in God.

To a genuine friend/ sister – Aleta McDowell. She never gave up on me no matter what. She is an authentic example of being a true friend. I will never forget her acts of love towards me or my children. She was the one who told me what God said about my baby when I had aborted her!

To my dad and mother, without you both, there would be no me! I love you both and I am glad that God chose you both to create me. In spite of what we've been through, I now know it was all working for my good! To all of my siblings: Patricia, Joanne(deceased), Louise(deceased) Laquita(deceased), Consie; I love you all.

To Pastor and Mother Rachel Collins. You were there often, showing me love when I wanted to give up, especially while I was pregnant. You continue to make sure that I cooked for Kayla. I love you, and Kayla does too!

To my coach Sophia! Thanks for being the example and motivator I need to push me into my purpose! To my CCL & CBK family! All of you hold a special place in my heart. You are my family indeed. Without you there will be no me.

To my cousin Aja Lomax. I love her dearly, and blood cannot make us any closer! No matter what, you are always there encouraging, pushing and supporting. I know that your love is genuine because I feel and see it; and for that I am so grateful. I am proud of you and can't wait to see all that God has for you. You are an awesome mother, friend, and cousin. I love you always, cuz! To my sister Tia! I love the love you have for me and Kayla. To my sister Jessica! I love you! I'm so happy to see what God is doing in your life. To my sister chantel and sister Paulette Harris! I miss you both so much! You both are in heaven now. Can't wait to see you there! To sis Pamela Harris. I love you.

Preface

Who will cry for the little girl!

Who will cry for the little girl so deep within me! Who will cry for the little girl who holds so much pain within!

Who will cry for the little girl who is afraid to come from behind that big black wall!

She fears the unknown because she doesn't know what it holds! She held her pain in so long that she learned to suppress the pain and hurt and even her fears!

She suppressed it with temporary fixes such as alcohol, drugs, sex, work, cutting herself, etc! Anything to take her mind off what's really on the inside!

She even learned how to wear a mask that no one can even recognize that she had on one.

She wears it so well that they think it's just her Normal feature! They don't even know that when she is alone at home she takes the mask off. So afraid to take it off fearing that others will hate the real her if they knew her real identity!

They don't know the abuse she suffered as a child, or the deep secrets she had to endure because she was told to "ssshhhh shhhhhh! Don't tell a soul!! It's our little secret!!"

But the secret was too much to endure that she hid behind the wall so deep inside and never ever came out again! The secret caused her to carry a muzzle on her mouth that made her lose her identity! See she didn't know that she had a protector all alone! In fact, she felt she was unloved and all alone. She didn't know she was fearfully and wonderfully made! She didn't realize that when your mother and father forsake you that she had a Heavenly Father who would take her up! Had she known, she would not be looking for love in others who only made her hide even more behind the wall so deep inside! One day though she found the love she was looking for all alone. She found the person who would cry for that little girl so deep inside!

He had already cried for that little girl inside; she just didn't know it. Not only that, but He had put all those tears that she cried for herself in a jar! He also had let her know that she was the APPLE of His eye! She no longer had to hide behind that black wall anymore! He wanted to dry up her tears and give her back her identity!! So you see I now know who will cry for the little girl who was so hidden inside of me!! JESUS, JESUS, JESUS will cry for me!! See he already did cry for me! Now my tears are replaced with abundant joy!

So if you happen to be that little girl or you may even be that little boy! Just know you have a Heavenly Father and big brother who wants to replace your sorrow with joy! And you too can come from behind that big black wall! (John 3:16)

Would my heart cry if it had an eye?

Have you ever been so hurt that it just seems like your heart is hurting so bad? It just seems like it's crying so deep within! The tears won't come out, yet you are crying so deep within.

It seems like your world is going through a whirlwind. You just can't seem to understand this pain. You get hits from all angles. Friends turning out not being friends! (yes, read it again) family is not close anymore. Finances going haywire. You keep getting misunderstood and you can't understand why. Why does this test have to be so hard? Well it seems hard because of the many hits the devil keeps throwing your way. Is my heart crying because the cry seems deep within? It gotta be my heart crying because the tears can't seem to flow from my eyes.

What about when you put your heart in someone only to find out the love you had for them was never the same love they had for you. Would your heart cry then? What about when it seems like no matter what you do your kids just don't get it. They keep acting up and you just don't understand why. Will your heart cry then? What about when you lose a loved one so special to you it seems like you can't go on, because you miss them so much! Will your heart cry then?

How about when it seems like your business is not going like you want it to? Or you may go through at the job? Or you just can't seem to lose or gain that weight you wanted to! Will your heart cry then! I ask God why can't my tears fall from my eyes and do my heart have an eye because it seems to be crying from within.

He had let me know that when I'm weak then I'm strong and that he catches my tears and puts them in a bottle. Oh wow! He is concerned about every hurt and pain that bothers us. He said he won't leave us ever and he is right here with us! So when it seems like we are alone we are not.

So when it seems like the tears can't come down your Face, I want you to ask yourself if your heart had an eye would it cry because mine did!

I am a prodigal daughter whose tears have a story!

However, the Lord showed me that He was there all the time, even when I felt all alone. He showed me my true identity and purpose. He showed me my tears were only there to push me into purpose.

And, Jesus brought me back to my rightful place in Him.

No, I am *not* flawless; neither am I completely perfect. But, I am definitely on my way up to God!

Contents

CONTENTS

1

Diamond In The Ruff

I don't really remember much about my toddler years; so, I often heard the stories about my younger years from my family. I was told, though, that I was abused by my mother, and that I was a very shy little girl who would hide whenever company came around.

I was also told that, at the age of two years old, my mother threw me down a flight of stairs. As a result, my arm was placed in a cast.

WOW! The devil was trying to destroy me, even at an early age! However, in spite of that incident, God didn't allow the devil to take my life.

You see, even though my mother did this to me, I love her dearly.

Don't get me wrong, I didn't always love my mother. In fact, I hated her guts and wished she was dead.

In fact, I even told people my mom was dead, even though she was alive and breathing. (That is another part of the story that I will get to later on in the story.)

I was told that at the age of three, I was trying to feed my little sister's food from the refrigerator.

(We were left at home without adult supervision quite often.)

It's amazing to me that I knew to feed my siblings at such a young age, seeing that I was a child myself.

I was burned many times with cigarettes, and I was physically abused. I was even abused by my mom's drunk boyfriends.

We were taken away from my mom because of an anonymous call to DCFS; we were left alone without adult supervision in the house for a couple of weeks this time. My little sister's pamper was so soaked until it was falling apart.

As a result, my siblings and I were separated; however, one of my sisters and I were placed in a foster home together.

My sister and I now lived with two ladies, Emma Beck and Lucille Beck. We were two frightened little girls, not knowing what the next chapter of our lives would be.

Siblings Issues

I was light skinned with long, black, coarse hair down my back. My sister was darker skinned with long, wavy hair down her back. My family has Cherokee Indian, British and African American in our blood.

My siblings all had nice, wavy hair, while mine was coarse and nappy. So, even as a child I stood out from my siblings because I was different. I was light complexioned while my siblings were dark complexioned. Although I do have a sister who was lighter than my dark-skinned siblings, she had a caramel complexion which is not as light as my complexion. Therefore, as you can imagine, I had to endure being called "honky" or "white girl" by my darker skinned siblings.

New Family

Miss Emma and Ms. Lucille were both elderly ladies who lived on the south side of Chicago. Ms. Lucille was nice, but Miss Emma was mean as a rattlesnake.

They had other foster children, two boys and a girl, but they were grown. The boys' names were Michael and Nate, and the girl's name was Lucille.

We soon became adjusted to our foster parents. They bought us whatever we wanted. To outsiders, it seemed like we were the perfect little family; but inside, we knew it was only a fairytale. We got beat morning, noon, and night!

Ms. Lucille was nice, but an alcoholic; but Miss Emma was as mean as a rattlesnake. I guess I got comfortable because, to tell you the truth, it's all I knew. So, I guess I figured being beat was normal: I was getting beat since my infant years.

Trouble Starts

Ms. Lucille had a boyfriend who we called "Poppa Speedy." He also was an alcoholic. He molested us when we were young. For some reason, he molested my sister more than me; I guess because I blocked out everything while he molested me.

He eventually stopped molesting me and continued to molest my little sister. He convinced our foster parents to let him take my little sister to school, pick her up from school and take her places. All the while, he was molesting her in his car.

> *Warning! This is why we have to be careful who we allow to be around our children. Don't allow children to go with just anybody. Even if you know the person, you must pray and ask God if the person is safe.*

The Search

As a little girl, and resulting from what I went through, I began to look for friends. In other words, I was trying to fit in.

I remember an incident where one of my friends asked me and my other friend to walk her home. I was seven years old. It was snowing really hard that day and it turned dark while we walked her home; so, we could not see how to get home to our houses from her house.

When we asked our friend to tell us how to get to our house, she told us to click our heels together three times and say "there's no place like home" and we would magically appear at our house.

Well, guess what? Yes, we did what she said! But, we were still at her house. So, we kept doing it thinking maybe we said it wrong; but, unfortunately, we were still there.

In fact, we were still there until 7 p.m.! Then, we began to cry. We knocked on our friend's door and asked her why it was not working. She told us that she had to go in the house because it was late, and closed the door in our face. Really!

Suddenly, my friend remembered how to get to her house. Once we reached her house, her mom asked me where I lived. Thankfully, I knew my address; I just didn't know how to get there. I'm so glad that her mom took me home.

But, oh boy did I get the worst whipping in the world when I got home that day! *This* time I had to strip butt naked.

Afterward, my little sister tried to ask me if I was okay, but I was too upset and cursed at her.

By this time, hatred was slowly creeping into my heart. I was angry because here I had trusted someone else, and they betrayed me again. And, once again, I suffered the consequences for that trust.

I realize now that the devil knew my future; so, he was setting up ways to plant seeds in me at an early age in order to try and destroy my life when I got older.

More Trauma

I remember going to one of my friend's house after school. She had an older brother who was a teenager. He would try to convince me to come into the closet with him where he was hiding. I would be so afraid until I would run out of her house every time he tried.

After he tried that a couple of times I decided to stop visiting her at her house.

And, I never forgot the school crossing guard who would try to get me to come to his house with him. I would run and scream all the way home!

Now, this man was an adult, but I was only seven years old. I mean the devil was really after me!

A lot of other things happened but I kind of blanked them out of my memory.

Better Home

I do remember there was a nice lady who lived next door to us who would let us come over sometimes. She had children, but they were older than us. She used to have Bible study in her house once a week.

One day, one of my foster mothers died. Since the other sister was too sick and too old to take care of us, she decided to send us back to foster care.

The nice lady who lived next door, Mrs. Berry, decided to take us instead of allowing us to return to foster care. I was so very happy because I really liked her and her family. So, my sister Joanne and I moved in with Mrs. Berry.

She had two girls and three boys. She also had another son, but he died in a tragic accident before we came to live with her.

Mrs. Berry would press our hair all the time. She always ate healthy, and had us drink healthy drinks.

Oh No!

I grew very close to Linlin, the oldest daughter. She was really nice to me. It seemed like I could tell her anything! She only got mad at me once. I remember it as though it was yesterday. She had just gotten in the house I guess. I got up and started walking towards my foster parent's room. I was actually sleepwalking. I didn't know what I was saying; but, when I came to myself, Linlin was fussing at me. (I'm laughing just thinking about this!)

I don't know what happened, but it must have been bad because she was very upset! I will never forget that night. (LOL!)

For some reason, my sister Joanne had to leave our house and go to another foster home. She was really crying, but for some reason I couldn't cry. I don't know why, but I was holding all my pain inside.

Yet, I did not understand why she had to leave. Linlin really helped comfort me about my sister having to leave. She let me know everything will be okay. It helped a little bit even though I was still hurt on the inside.

Church Life

My foster mom used to take me to church on the south side. I think the name of the church was South Shore Baptist Church. While there, I won first prize for writing a poem about Jesus! I really liked going to Sunday school too.

More Trouble

There was another incident that happened when I was seven years old. It is in my memory as clear as day!

A girl who was 12 years old started coming to our church that week – we called her Lele. It was a Tuesday night and we were having Bible class. She had just been released from a mental institute. She was admitted into the mental facility because she constantly punched out windows with her bare hands. I was told that, one time it took five men from our church to hold her down while she was having a mental encounter.

Well, one day they brought her to our Bible study class that was held in the basement. The adults were upstairs. Our class was from the ages 6 to 8 years old. Mrs. Berry, along with another lady (I don't remember the other lady's name), was the Bible study's teacher.

The other lady brought Lele into our classroom. I remember thinking, "Why is this teen girl in our class?" But, I didn't know this was the same girl that everyone was talking about. During the bible class, we sang a song that said" Making Jesus number one." Lele said in a deep, manly voice, "Making satan number one."

Now mind you, I had just watched the movie *Exorcist* two weeks prior to this; so, I was already terrified of the movie! But, when I saw this, I was really horrified!

Mrs. Berry and the other teacher began saying, "We love Lele." Out of Lele's mouth in the same deep, manly voice, she began saying, "We hate Lele and we are going to kill her."

Now, all of the children in the bible class began to cry, including me. We were really scared!

It was time for us to take a bathroom break. As I went to the bathroom, Lele was at the water fountain. I continued to go towards her where the bathroom was, and she started to talk out again. Yes, she was possessed by demons.

7

I took off running while screaming back to the classroom. I wanted to go home. Needless to say, I did *not* want to come back to the church anymore. I did not feel safe since even the pastor could not hold her down whenever she got into that rage.

Later, I was told that she got possessed by going to a fortune teller/psychic.

> *Warning! We have to be careful and stay clear of all of satan's evil devices, such as fortune tellers, psychics, etc. These vices open a spiritually satanic door that we do not ever want to open! It opens up legal doors with satan.*

Yet another incident was concerning a certain man on our block where I lived. Everyone loved this man. He seemed really nice to me. He always allowed the children on the block to mow his lawn and clean his yard, then rewarded them with candy and gifts.

Well, one day he said he was going to take the girls to cheerleading practice. My foster mother was really strict with me and I wasn't allowed to do a lot of things nor go anywhere.

A lot of my friends were able to do many things I could not do. I really wanted to be a cheerleader; therefore, I decided that this time I will go and not let my foster mom know. I put my bike in the backyard and ran off with my friends.

We all went with the man to go to cheerleading practice. When we arrived at the place, we were told to take off our shoes. People were there on their knees, and they all had on these white robes with hoods. There was an altar in the middle of the room and some candles burning around the altar. The people were chanting words that kept playing in my head.

I blocked out of my memory most of this incident, and can't remember all of the details. But, I do remember that I heard a voice clear as day say to me "RUN!!!" And, I tell you *I RAN!*

Deceiving Looks

I don't remember if I warned my friends, how I got away from there or how I found my house. All I remember is I clearly heard that voice say *RUN* and *I Ran!*

These experiences are very real and the reasons why I have been strict with my own children. This should help children see why it's so important to let their parents know their whereabouts!

I realize that, if something bad had happened to me, nobody would've known where I was because I didn't let my guardian know.

As Parents, someone seeming nice doesn't mean we should let our children be or go with them. Ask and seek God about people that you do and do not know.

This man appearing to be nice encouraged the other parents to allow their children to go with him. They didn't have a clue that this man was actually a devil worshiper! He wanted to sacrifice all of us to Satan. Please know that looks can be very deceiving.

The Bible says in first Samuel 16 verse 7 that the Lord does not see as man sees, but the Lord looks at the heart. "But the Lord said unto Samuel, Look not on his countenance or on the height of his stature; because I have refused him: for the Lord seeth not as man seeth; for man looketh on the outward appearance, but the Lord looketh on the heart." We must ask God to allow us to see the hearts of people. After that experience, I had constant dreams of what happened.

Even though I didn't really know what was going on at that place, for some reason I knew it just wasn't right. And, I even knew somehow the chanting that was playing in my head just wasn't right either. Therefore, every time it played in my head, I would cry out, "Please take it out of my head!" God did just that too! He took those thoughts out of my head. I wasn't listening to them anymore! Praise God!

After that day, I knew not to go with that man anymore

2

Seeds planted!

The Visit!

I had my own room and two beds were in it; so, I had to share my room with my foster mom's mother whenever she visited.

I remember one night while I was sitting in my bed, she was sitting on her bed, and just kept telling me that I was ugly and stupid, and that I would never amount to anything.

I would cry until I cried myself to sleep. For some reason, I never told my foster mom what was said. I just dealt with it by wishing I was dead.

As I think about it now, I realize that the enemy was trying to plant a seed into me to destroy my life right there!

Fortunately, she didn't live with us; she only visited from time to time. But every time she came, she would speak those negative words to me constantly.

Since I already had gone through similar experiences, this only helped make my self- esteem even lower.

Even though I was a pretty little girl, I felt really ugly and alone. I was constantly trying to please people.

Seeking Love

Two of my foster brothers were very nice to me, though. My brother Jade was my favorite. He would take me places with him, and he spent time with me. He bought me things, which really made me feel like I was special.

I truly hated when Jade went away to the Navy because I knew that I would no longer feel that brotherly love that he gave me. His brotherly love was the satisfaction to the void that I needed to fill. It was a father void that was missing.

I had another foster brother named Ben who was really nice to me as well. It felt like he was my *big* brother. He never made me feel like I was different. He treated me as if I was his *real* little sister.

Ben and his wife always took me places. But, all of that stopped when they finally had their own daughter. Her name was winter. She was a pretty little girl, and I loved her greatly.

I was really excited to be an aunt! I played with her often. However, when I would see her sitting on her dad's lap playing, I would suddenly get jealous and pinch her while she was sitting and playing on her dad's lap. Her dad would always wonder why she was crying.

One day I tried to pinch her again. But, this time I accidentally pinched her dad instead! Boy, I was so embarrassed and hurt! I got into trouble that day.

(Laughing to myself and shaking my head at myself as I'm writing this. Shame on me!)

I understand now that I was only acting out of anger at the fact that I missed the attention my brother gave me. I was jealous because, after his baby was born, Ben stopped taking me places and spending time with me.

Now seeking attention and love, I began to hang outside more. I found myself stealing from my foster mom. But, I didn't even *have to* steal because she always gave me allowance!

I would buy my friends whatever they wanted at the candy store. Trying to fit in made me do a lot of things. This was the beginning of my trying to please people.

Beginning of fear!

As a youth, I was terrified of drunk men. So much so until, when my foster mom would send me and my sisters to the corner store, if I saw a drunk man in front of the store, I wouldn't go in. I would just start crying in front of the store. (I know it's weird, right? Shaking my head).

Then, my sisters and I would run home. My foster mom would try to send me back to the store to go get what she requested, but I would not go. I would just start screaming and hollering real loud. I didn't even care if she whipped me. I was too terrified to go where drunk men were.

Once, there were some twins who were older in their teens; they let us play with their dollhouse for a couple of days. When we finally had to return it, my sister and I went around the corner to their items. When we got to their house, one of the twins informed us that we had forgotten some of the pieces.

So, as we were walking back, I noticed a drunk man on the other side of the street. He was just walking and minding his own business. I started screaming and hollering. I was halfway to the twins house. Instead of running to their house, I just threw the pieces into the snow and ran back home.

When I got home, I lied and told my foster mom that I took the pieces back.

Honestly, I didn't care if I would have gotten a whipping: I was too scared to go back. I actually would rather have gotten a whipping than be made to go back near where that drunk man was!

Scared Straight

I had blocked out a lot of my childhood because it was so painful. But, I was glad to have Linlin in my life though. She always treated me as a *real* sister. I could talk to her about anything.

I went outside a lot to play with the other children who lived on the block. They used to play strange games, like "Catch a girl, Freak a girl." Some of them would actually have grown-up sex!

I was terrified of this game! My foster mom made me so scared of it. She made it plain and clear that she would know if I did. I never ever tried it either.

So, when the other children were playing this game I would run on my porch and sit down. My heart would be beating really hard and fast too.

One of the boys wanted me to play the game with him really badly. He would tell me often that he was going to *get me* one day. Now, that used to really scare me!

Good Times

Those same friends also rode around on bikes, which was fun.

Sadly, some of my friends did get pregnant though, which, to me, was kind of weird since they were so young – ages 9 to 13.

One day, I met a friend named Marlo who became my best friend. When I got my allowance, I would split my money with her.

I didn't want to play the games that the other children on my block were playing. So, instead, I chose to play with Marlo; and she and I became very close like sisters. I even began to sneak over to her house to play with her.

I can only remember one time that we got upset with each other. Afterward, we were back to being buddies.

Separation Anxiety

Then one day, my foster mother told me that my caseworker found a family member who wanted to get me.

I was shocked, seeing that I had never heard of this *family member* before.

I remember my aunt Madea since I had visited her from time to time. I was also in touch with my sister Patricia from time to time; but, I had never heard of *this* family member.

When I heard this from my foster mother, I was very angry and sad that I would have to leave. I loved my foster family and they were all I knew!

I cried so hard that day. I just really didn't know who this lady was! Why did she want me all of a sudden? Didn't she know I loved where I lived? How dare she want me now! Why couldn't she just leave me alone?

I was crying and started telling my foster mom, "I'm sorry for stealing and being bad!" I felt like the reason for me having to leave must have been something I did wrong.

The day that my caseworker came to take me away, I cried like a baby. I was leaving behind my best friend, my other friends, my first childhood crush (at my school), and my family who I had grown to love.

Well, needless to say, that drive with my caseworker seemed extremely long.

Another Home

My caseworker took me to Joliet where I would live with my Aunt. I didn't really know my Aunt and her family because I was with my foster family up until I was 11 years old.

In the house lived my Aunt, her two children (my cousins), my brother, and two of my sisters. One of my cousins was in college; so, most of the time there was only one of my cousins in the house.

My Aunt was fun, but kind of strict. The good part is that I did get introduced to more of my family who I had never met before.

I met my grandfather, grandmother, some aunts, uncles, and some more cousins. I was glad about meeting these family members because I didn't know about my family since I was living in foster homes for quite some time.

No Emotion

During this time, I even got to visit my mom. It was strange because I had forgotten that I had a real mom since I was always in foster homes.

I would feel bad and even sad whenever I saw others with their moms; I wished it was me with my mom.

So, when I met my mom, I didn't know *what* to feel since I had forgotten her. And, as I stated earlier, I had blocked my mom out of my memory; that was my way of blocking out some of the tragedies I experienced as a youth when I was living with my mom.

Tragedy Again

I was finally happy since I was starting to cope with living with my other family members. It was a strange environment, but I tried to get used to it.

I loved it when we would go visit my Aunt who lived in the Robert Taylor Homes. I really liked her a lot!

But, one day we learned of a bad tragedy that happened to my Aunt's daughter: my little cousin was found on the railroad tracks dead, naked and wrapped in a sheet.

The family was devastated!

I cried so hard; and I listened to one of her favorite songs by Debarge to remember her.

I could not understand why someone would do this to her. Well, I later found out that my favorite relative whom I loved very dearly was the one who did this to her. He had raped and killed her.

I was extremely terrified when I found out that my favorite relative had done this horrible thing. I couldn't believe he did this to her! *Not my favorite relative!* This had to be wrong; at least that's what I kept telling myself.

Actually, I was in shock because I realized that it could have been me. I would have gone anywhere with this relative because he was my favorite!

I really thought he was nice. I never would have thought he was capable of doing any harm to me or anyone else. But, it seems that his actions were a result of the things he had suffered when he was growing up.

Even worse, this incident caused a great division in my family. We were already divided; but, this caused even more division.

On top of that, as if this tragedy was not bad enough, my aunt started playing a strange game with all of my sisters and brother! I was so horrified by this game until I would lock myself in the bathroom when they would play this game. I never played a game like this before in foster homes.

Why Here

I was so angry at my caseworker for bringing me here. Whenever my aunt would knock on the door telling me to come out, I would start panicking. I would open up the bathroom window and jump out of it.

I often ran away to my Aunt Earlene's house. She was the best in the world, and I loved her dearly!

I used to tell Aunt Earlene what was going on at the house where I stayed, and that I didn't want to go back. She never made me leave though. She always just let me stay there until my aunt came to get me.

Then, once my Aunt came to get me, Aunt Earlene would tell my Aunt to stop making me do those things.

Of course, my aunt would deny that what I told my Aunt Earlene was true. However, once we got back home, my aunt would go back to trying to play the game again.

Regardless of what might happen, under no circumstances was I going to play those crazy games! I didn't care if she beat me! I refused to play those games with her; so, I would constantly run away to avoid playing those games. Also, my sister and I used to go play outside.

Now This

We began to hang out with a couple of guys at their house. I only went to their house to get away from the madness at my house. One of the boys liked me, and the other one liked my sister. The one guy who liked me wanted to have sex with me. But, I didn't want to have sex; so, I refused his attempts. I just wanted companionship and a listening ear. Whew!

My sister and I were wards of the state; therefore, we couldn't sleep in the same bed. There was only one bed in the girls room; so, we would take turns with one sleeping in the bed while the other would sleep on the couch.

Well, one week it was my turn to sleep on the couch. While I was sleeping, I suddenly felt someone on top of me trying to pull my clothes off. I woke up terrified! I began screaming really loud as my heart was beating really fast.

It was my cousin who was doing this. He told me he was sorry, and that he thought I was my sister (as though that makes what he was doing okay).

17

I said, "That's my sister and your cousin!" This was really sick; I couldn't believe my ears! I began to think to myself, "How long has this been going on?"

I was now even more angry with my caseworker. I was so angry at her for making me leave my lovely home and new family to come to this type of craziness in this house! It just didn't seem fair that I had to be here.

Well, my Aunt woke up because of all the screaming and found out what my cousin had done. After I told her what had happened, she told me to go to bed and not to say anything else about it. She said that it will be okay.

I thought to myself, "Is that all she is going to do?" That night, I went to bed so scared. I was too scared to go to bed that night.

Life Continues

Well, my sister and I continued to switch sleeping spots every week. But now, when it was my week to sleep on the couch, I barely slept, and I put on three pairs of pants and three shirts to sleep in. I thought that all the clothes would make him have a hard time pulling them off without me waking up.

Boy, was I depressed! So, one day I called my foster sister Linda and told her what happened. She was shocked! She comforted me and let me know that I needed to tell someone. But, I felt that I *couldn't* tell anyone because I was afraid that I would get one of the beatings that my aunt used to give us.

Being wards of the state, we had to go to counselors. One day when we went to our counselor, I asked mine would she make sure she didn't say a word if I told her a secret. She said Yes. So, I told her what had happened to me because it was really bothering me; I was terrified to sleep at night and afraid of what might happen.

Three days after I told my counselor, some people came to see me and my siblings at our school. They asked us about the incidents that happened at my aunt's house.

They took us out of school that day and took us to our house to get our things. We were *finally* leaving that house!

My aunt screamed at me and said that it was all my fault that we were leaving. She repeatedly said this to my brother and sisters. I began to cry because I thought that it was my fault. I thought to myself, "If only I kept my mouth shut!"

All Regrets

I began to get angry at my counselor for telling on me. I was thinking to myself, "She promised not to say anything!"

As tears fell down my cheeks, I vowed that I would no longer reveal any secrets about me anymore! That was the beginning of how I started keeping stuff inside. I never would tell anyone how I felt.

I was so hurt because it felt as if all of my siblings were angry at me for telling. My heart was hurting so bad; but, yet I was relieved that I wouldn't have to go through what I went through anymore.

3

It's Educational

Well, after this we went to our other aunt's house, Mimi. I was kind of fond of Aunt Mimi since I used to visit her from time to time. She would take us to visit our mom while our mom was in jail.

I remember that my mom was in Dwight Correctional Center. When we visited, my mom would always try to kiss me on my cheek; and I hated that because it felt too mushy.

Aunt Mimi lived on the West side of Chicago. Although I was raised on the south side, when I was young and moved to Joliet I became a little suburban girl! I was in eighth grade.

Getting Educated

When I was graduating from eighth grade, I went to Hefferan School. I was really shy in school so I kept to myself. Not many boys liked me; I guess I was a need for them.

After I graduated, I just sat on my porch during the summer. I had some friends who lived upstairs from us named the Moores family. We would get into disagreements and fights sometimes, but we soon became good friends.

One of my older cousins didn't like me because of my skin color. Due to her feelings about me, she lied on me by telling Aunt Madea that I was having sex with my friend's dad.

Unfortunately, Aunt Mimi believed my cousin. I couldn't believe that she lied to me. I was so mad! Although my friend's dad told Aunt Mimi that was not true, she still believed my cousin. Due to this lie that my cousin told about me, I was no longer allowed upstairs. I also was beaten really badly about the lie. I was so hurt! How could Madea believe this lie that was told about me!

> *Warning: Parents, use wisdom when told something about your children. Pray about it! Trust me: God will give you the wisdom on how to handle all situations. We must learn to listen to our children!*

Another Tragedy

One day, I got into an altercation with another girl. I don't remember why, but she wanted to fight me. She even had an ax to hit me with. But fortunately, a guy named Wood defended me and chased the girl away. This was the start of a relationship between Wood and me. I felt like he was my *prince charming*.

I never experienced anyone taking up for me and defending me. I was longing for love, and I felt this must have been love; at least, that's what I thought! We called ourselves so in-love.

> *Warning: Ladies, don't get love confused with lust!*

My sister Joanne and I had started hanging out with some new friends – Trina and Diana. I had stopped being at my house so much to avoid all of the drama there.

For example, my older cousin (who I will call T) used to beat me for no reason at all sometimes! Once, she thought I had done something to her son. Boy, did she beat me that day! And, Aunt Mimi just watched while doing nothing at all about her beating me.

I got really depressed about that until I decided to take my own life. I went to the bathroom, took two big bottles of pills and some Nyquil that I had found in the medicine cabinet. I tried to hide the empty bottles under the sink cabinet. I started feeling sleepy, so I went to my room and laid down.

I don't know how my sister and brother knew what I did, but they went to Aunt Madea and told on me. The next thing I knew, Aunt Mimi came out of her room yelling and saying she was gonna teach me how to kill myself, since I wanted to take my life.

As a result, instead of taking me to the hospital for all the pills and medicine that I had taken, she took us to our grandma's house. Now, this puzzled me because I couldn't figure out why she didn't take me to the hospital!

I don't know why we even went to my grandma's house since I was afraid of my grandma. She seemed like she was possessed with demons! (Yes I said I was possessed with demons! In spite of what you may think, demons are very real!)

She always had this really scary look on her face that frightened me. But, once we got there, I was so sleepy until I could not even keep my eyes open! I kept falling asleep.

I thank God every time I think about this because I *should* be dead! I didn't go to the hospital to get my stomach pumped of the pills and Nyquil that I took; but, God spared my life!

I didn't wake up until the next morning; but I found out I was at home.

New Flash: In spite of the plans of satan, God had bigger plans for my life. Guess what satan! You lost again!

Real Love

I started going to see Wood more often. I felt that he was the only one who really loved me.

Well, the day finally came when Wood wanted to have sex. I was only fondled a lot when I was much younger. I was never penetrated by my abusers; only touched by their hands, rubbed on with their private part, and other things that are too horrible to describe. So, I was still a virgin.

I went to Wood's house as I usually did. Then, one day when I got there, he said, "If you love me, you will have sex with me." He said that he was in love and wanted to prove his love for me. I was really scared, but I didn't want to lose him. I was so terrified, but yet I wanted to please him.

I felt as though I had to have sex with him so he would know that my love was real. I felt I had to show him that I really loved him; or, so I thought. It was really lust.

I finally said, Yes. We decided to have sex when his mom went downstairs. It hurt so bad! I was thinking to myself how could this be a good thing that hurts like this? I was thinking to myself that I didn't want to do this anymore!

Fortunately, his mom came upstairs and knocked on the door. He told me to hide in his closet. He then opened the door and his mom came into the room and looked around to see what was going on. I was *so* scared!

His mom found me in the closet and told me to go home. Boy, was I embarrassed; I couldn't look her in the face! I hurried out the door and Wood walked me home.

I was hurting really bad and bleeding in my private area. I kept thinking to myself, "Boy, love sure does hurt!"

I thought us having sex was love. I didn't know that I was giving him my mind, soul and body.

23

> *Warning: OK! Do you know that once you give a guy your body, he becomes a big part of you; especially the first guy. You all become soul ties*

He really had my mind! I was constantly going to Wood's house now. Aunt Mimi didn't allow *me* to have company at our house (or boys calls), but Wood's mom allowed him to have company at his house.

Aunt Mimi didn't allow me to have boys' calls either. So, Wood would have his sister call my house and ask for me.

Wood would tell me that he loved me. Hearing him say that made me feel so happy because it seemed like he had filled the void that was in my heart! (But, in reality, Wood didn't love me.)

I would stay over his house until the street lights came on. Then, we would sneak into the basement to have sex. Even though it hurt *very badly* and I really didn't care about having sex, I continued since I wanted to please him.

Next Phase

I started smoking weed (marijuana) with my sister and our friends, Diana and Trina. Since there was always drama at home, it felt good to hang out with them, or Wood.

> *Warning: You must know that, once the devil gets you in his trap, he will eventually take off his cover and reveal himself.*

Well, that's exactly what happened: the cover was taken off. My *prince* charming whom I thought was my life had started to beat me. Yep, I found myself in an abusive relationship with him! And, of course I really started smoking weed even more!

I already had a whole lot of crazy stuff going on at home: incest, witchcraft being worked on us, etc. Now, I had to deal with this abuse too! It was too stressful right now. And mind you, I was just a teenager trying to deal with all of these problems!

Although he was beating me, I still loved him for some reason. I felt that maybe I deserve to be beaten since he loved me and was only jealous.

I actually *thought* this was love, and no one could tell me different. My friends used to try to talk to me about it, but I would say that He was my "baby" and I loved him no matter what.

News Flash: This is the kind of thing that happens when you are looking for love in the wrong places. To the young ladies reading this, please know that God loves you even if it feels like no one else does. Getting abused is not love. If you are in an abusive relationship, get out quickly!

The devil only wants to beat you down and make you have low self-esteem. In case you don't know who, you are, you are an heir! You are the daughter of a King which makes you a princess. So, never settle for less because you are royalty since your father God is your King.

4

Misguided

I never knew who I was; so, I settled for anything! I didn't know that I was royalty.

Aunt Mimi used to send us to church on Sundays; but, I eventually stopped going. I would say to myself "Why am I going to church? (Aunt) Madea goes to church all the time and she is just like me: we both curse and do other sins. So, what's the point of us going to church?"

I would see my aunt be one way in church; and, out of church, she was a whole different way. So, I didn't see a need to go to church if it didn't change you.

I really didn't know a lot about God; only a little bit that I learned from my foster mom, Mrs. Berry.

I went to church with my aunt in Joliet as well; but, there was so much *craziness* until I really didn't see a difference between the people in the church and the people in the world. Even the pastor's daughter was having sex in the church in Joliet!

Once, Aunt Mimi took us to a service where the minister was named Prophet Wond. He wore a lot of gold jewelry, and always had us get in line for prayer. Since I saw people falling out on the floor when they received prayer, when he prayed for me, I fell out too! LOL

Of course, I was faking though! I would stay for a minute on the floor, then peek to make sure no one was looking at me, and then get up.

But, my aunt used to give Prophet Wond all of her money. We would stay for long periods at his church. Something just didn't seem right with this man to me though!

I just never saw anyone who I felt was really close to God. Whenever my sister and brother went to those services, I would go to Wood's house. And, I would threaten my siblings not to tell Aunt Madea. Then, when church was over, they would come and pick me up from Wood's house to go home.

Aunt Madea always gave us money for offerings, but we would spend it at the store. God, *please* forgive me for stealing! But, I didn't know I was stealing from God at the time. I *did* know that I had no desire to be saved.

Father's Crush

Well, as any child would, I kept asking my aunt about my dad. I really wanted to know who he was. I longed for a dad all of my life. I felt like my life would be complete if I found him.

One day Aunt Mimi finally got the information about my dad. took me to his house. Now, how crazy is it that my dad's house was only a couple of blocks away from my house? All this time my dad was close by and I did not even know it!

Aunt Mimi took me to my dad's house, which happened to be my grandad's house. My grandad was happy to see me. I was so happy, and my granddad was so nice to me! He gave me my dad's address which was in the Hornet projects. He lived there with his girlfriend and children.

I called and went over to his house, but he wasn't there. While I was there, I met my four sisters and his girlfriend.

Of course, he has more daughters though. My half-sister took me around his job. We called him on the phone, and he told me that he didn't want me to know where he worked because he didn't want my mom to pursue child support. That crushed my heart!

Although inside of me my soul was crushed, I kept smiling because I did not want my half-sister to see how hurt I was.

I didn't care about any *child support*. Didn't he know that I had waited my whole life to meet him? *Child support* was the *last* thing on my mind! I always imagined a different meeting between us.

My dad did smile when he saw me, but I didn't get any hugs or kisses from him. I didn't get any excitement that his long-lost daughter was finally in his life. In spite of the disappointment, I did start visiting more

Seeking Dad

Since I didn't get the attention I wanted and desperately needed from my dad, I looked for it guys. That's when Wood and I became even closer. I felt that the love that I couldn't get from my dad I'll get from Wood. I needed Wood to fill that void that was in my heart.

Now, I started going to high school. I was at Schurz high school, an ethnically mixed school, and I hated it! I had no friends there. My aunt had put me in Schurz in hopes that I would not get involved in any crazy stuff.

I did finally have two friends, a boy and a girl. I was really shy, so I hardly talked to anyone. And even worse, I had old looking clothes because my aunt never brought us any new clothes; so, I was a homely looking girl.

I used to steal candy from the store since I never got any spending money. I would sometimes spend my car fare on junk food, and then I would ask strangers for money to have transportation so I could get on the bus to go home. How crazy was that!

Our clothes always came from the thrift store. Now, nothing is wrong with buying clothes from the thrift store, but a child shouldn't look like an old grandma, especially in their teenage years! We only got new things every blue moon from a store called Goldblatt's.

One year, while school was out because of a strike, my aunt had enrolled us in the Marillac House boys and girls club for youth. I will never forget this day ever.

My half-sister, Joanne(sister), Louise(sister), Consie (brother) and I went into a store before we went to the club. *They* all stole outfits and shoes; I was the only one too scared to steal clothes and shoes. I thought stealing candy was different, and I didn't want to go to jail. So, I never stole from the stores.

But, I wanted some clothes and shoes too, so I asked them if they would get me something. They said they would not, and that I had to get it myself. I got mad at them for not getting me anything; so, when we got home that day, I told them. They were so mad at me! They wouldn't talk to me that day.

Grandma shoes!

The next day, Aunt Mimi made me put on some really ugly boots. They looked like shoes that someone who was 100 years old would wear!

I was crying so hard and asking her to please not make me wear them, but she didn't care. She still made me wear them. I was so embarrassed!

My sisters and brother were still mad at me, so they were not talking to me at all. When we got to the club, I tried to hide my boots behind a chair. Some children still noticed the ugly boots, and talked about my shoes really bad, embarrassing me even more!

I then tried to make back up with my sisters and brother. At first, they were laughing at me too! But, we eventually made up.

As soon as I got home, I went to the basement and hid those shoes in some coals that we had in the basement! After that, whenever Aunt Mimi asked where those boots were, I lied and said I didn't know. I really didn't care if she would have beat me about those boots if she found out I was lying; anything was better than wearing those ugly boots!

She would buy me flowered dresses that I thought were ugly; so, I could not wait to buy my own clothes!

Better Living

Since I kept ditching classes, Aunt Mimi decided to put me in Marshall High School. This school was closer to my house.

I wanted to go to Marshall High School anyway because I would be around people that I knew. I was so happy! And, sure enough, as soon as I started, I saw people who I knew; and, I met new people as well! It seemed like it was now easier for me to make new friends.

And, since I had a summer job, I was able to buy myself some clothes!

School is really fun to me now. I started hanging with the popular crowd. We would ditch classes and go to the lunchroom.

> *Warning: I wished I knew then that education was important, and far better than ditching classes!*

Why This

A lot of my boyfriend's friends attended Marshall High School as well. But, I never cheat on my boyfriend, although he always cheated on me. I was so *in love*, so I thought.

Well, one boy named Billy liked me, but I was just friends with him. I never looked at him as a boyfriend; only as a friend. He knew I had a boyfriend, so he didn't try to push our friendship into anything more than that.

One day, Billy tried to sit on my lap, but I pushed him off. I didn't think anything about this at the time; I just brushed it off.

Well, after that day, Wood came to my house. He had some guys with him, but I didn't think anything was wrong; I was just happy to see him.

When I came outside to see what he wanted, he told me to walk into the gangway by my house.

When we walked into the gangway, he started hitting me with his fists, kicking me and flipping me on the concrete! Mind you, I'm only 5'0" and he was like 6'3" tall!

I truly didn't understand what was going on! He said that I knew why, but I didn't. Then, his friend Deon said that I was kissing that boy named Billy.

I was so mad because it was a lie! I couldn't believe that he lied in my face.

My aunt finally came outside to see what was going on, Thank God! Because he stopped hitting me. So, I went inside the house. I was in such a rage!

I headed straight out the back door to go to my dad's house. I thought that maybe he could save me from this guy. As soon as I opened the gate, my aunt had called out to Wood and told him I was leaving. I felt so betrayed by my aunt!

I finally just went to my room and wrote in my journal. I hated all of them, and I felt so alone. Tears flowed down my face as always! I was sad and I felt so alone. Why was my life like this! I could not understand why bad things were always happening to me.

How could my aunt be on his side when she clearly saw that my nose was busted and my eye was swollen? How could someone who claimed to love you treat you so badly?

> *Warning: Remember young ladies, abuse is not love. Never let anyone put their hands on you to physically harm you. If they have physically harmed you, get out of that relationship quickly.*

It got to the point where I began to feel like that was love. I started believing that guys beat you if they really love you. I felt like I had to accept this because this was true love, wasn't it?

He did a lot of bad things; such as having sex with my close friends and my cousin. Yet, I still felt that he loved me.

> *Warning: See, when you don't value yourself as the princess or queen God made you, you will accept anything. Get to know who you are! God says we are fearfully and wonderfully made by Him.*

New Love

Soon, my aunt put me out of the house because I constantly missed curfew. So, I went to stay with my half-sister.

My half-sister began to show me *the ropes* around the Hornet projects. Yes, I was still *in love* with Wood, but I was tired of the beatings and the cheatings. So, I had stopped talking to him while I was at my sister's house.

Now, I met this guy named Shawn. I was really *digging* him! He looked like one of the guys of the group New Edition. Shawn and his friends even did talent shows performing as New Edition. Since I was looking for love, I felt like he could fill the void I felt.

We would go to his house and have sex in his mom's waterbed. (Waterbeds were a big thing back then.) I started going with him everyday; and my half-sister had her own thing going on too.

Shawn and his friends used to win trophies for their performances. Of course, since they started getting recognition, the girls started liking them.

Shawn started selling drugs; so, he started seeing other girls. Since he was doing wrong, I started trying to do other stuff too.

I decided to start going to the teenage clubs with my half-sister; it was one called The Factory and open on Saturday nights. My half-sister and I went every Saturday. We would even steal money from her mom's candy store in order to have money to go to the club. Her mom didn't notice since she made lots of profit every day.

I started liking The Factory! It was a place to meet new people.

I met a guy called Wayne there. He was a friend of my friend Pp, my best friend at the time. Wayne was from the Rockwell projects; so, we would go visit the Rockwell projects all the time. It was as if the Hornets girls were visiting the Rockwell guys.

Unforeseen Dangers

Pp and I started hanging with them a lot. We also started smoking weed with Wayne and Billy. One day, they gave us leaf (it's a drug) instead of weed; of course we did not know it though. I was *so* naive at the time until I really thought it was weed.

I suddenly felt kind of weird, and I kept crying. Pp started acting weird too, and making sounds like a witch. I ran all the way home to the Hornets projects from Rockwell projects at 2:00am!

When I got home, I kept telling My half- sister that Pp had turned into a witch. My head was spinning, so I laid down and went to sleep. The next morning, my half- sister told me how I was acting. I was shocked. That's when I realized that they had given us some leaf (a drug) instead of weed. I was as mad as ever! I never smoked with him or them again!

I later found out that he was with another girl called E. (E and I later became friends; she turned out to be really nice!

Then, I had started to hang with the *Gangster Stones*. My naive self had even put a tattoo on my body that said *Gangster Stone*. My younger sister and I joined this gang together. I only joined because I wanted to be popular.

Since I was a runaway, my aunt would constantly have to search for me. And, she would always send the police to my step-mom's house. My step-mom got tired of the police coming to her house; so, she told me that I had to leave.

I then began to stay in the Trap houses that the Gangster Stones had. I also stayed at Wayne's house a lot. Sometimes, if he was asleep when I got there, his sister would let me in the house. When he woke up, I would be in his bed.

My friends that I was with started *"boosting"* (stealing) clothes and food. I still was too afraid to do this because I was afraid of going to jail!

One day, I stole a package of meat and got caught by the security guard. The security guard scared me by telling me I was going to go to jail! I was crying really hard and told him I was sorry. He did let me go home. And, boy did I run out of that store! I never stole again; items, that is.

5

Just Existing

One day, some of my friends, Wayne and his friends and I were all standing outside. Wayne's ex-girlfriend got into an altercation with one of the guys. So, Wayne got mad and defended her.

I was shocked! How could he do this for her in my presence? I was so hurt until I just walked off. After that, it was over between us because *that* was the last straw. He kept calling me afterwards, but I just ignored his calls. I cried so hard about that incident until my hurt turned into rage.

But a short while later, my friend and her guy called Wayne on the phone. They tricked us both and got us back together.

I went back to him because I really cared for him. But, I felt that I had to pay him back for that incident, though. So, I had my ex-boyfriend come and walk with me to the building. He was hugging me, and I was smiling really hard.

Wayne got so angry! Once my ex-boyfriend left, Wayne picked me up and put me in the garbage can. Now, I was mad, and embarrassed!

My half-sister was mad too. We got someone to confront Wayne about putting me in the garbage can. But, of course I went back to him.

The last day I was with Wayne, I had a slight accident on myself and got caught after curfew by the police. While in custody, the police found out that I was a run-away, and put me into a group home out South. I forget exactly where it was, but I do remember that it was by the lake.

The staff was very nice, but they let us have our way. We were allowed to go out every day and buy weed to smoke. When we returned to the group home, we were higher than high.

One day, I ate a rotten peach; but, I was so high until it didn't matter that it was rotten.

Lessons Learned

The group home residents were girls of all ages and nationalities. We really didn't have any restrictions there. We only had to come home on time.

Once, one of the girls asked me to take a walk with her. She went to meet some guy. It turned out he was a pimp, and I think he was pimping her. She wanted me to come with her to try to recruit me for him.

When I realized what was going on, I started screaming at the top of my lungs! He became angry and hit the girl for bringing me. He told her to take my crazy behind back where I came from. Never again did I go anywhere else with her!

Oftentimes, the other girls and I would go to the lake and walk on the ice; of course, we were high off weed. That was crazy because we could have fallen into the water.

The group home staff knew we were high, but they never said anything.

I even caught crabs from using the toilets in the group home. [Note: "Crabs" is a disease that shows on your genitals and is usually contracted through intercourse, sitting on toilets that are not disinfected or using an infected person's towel.] I guess one of the girls had the disease and spread it since the toilets were rarely cleaned thoroughly.

I got homesick and began crying. Seeking comfort, I decided that I would go see Wayne. So, I ran away from the group home to go see him. It was actually good that I ran away. I found out later that, after I left the group home, the girls/residents and the staff got raped by neighbors living next door to the group home. Learning this made me so glad that I had left when I did.

Well, now I am back at my step-mom's house. But, my aunt kept calling the police to find me; so I had to leave again.

Since I now had nowhere else to go, I went back with the Gangster Stones. I thought that rejoining was the only choice I had so I could have shelter when the night came.

All we did was go to stores and steal. I *still* was too scared to steal since I got caught that one time. Now, I found myself sleeping in drug houses. Although I was scared, I felt that I had nowhere else to go.

I couldn't go back to my step-mom's house because she no longer wanted me there. I now understand that she just didn't want to lose her apartment by harboring a runaway.

Back then, I didn't understand this at all, and it only added to the rejection I felt so deep inside.

Wanting Nurturing

I longed for a mother's love, but I could never find anyone to love me like that.

My step-mom never really loved me, and never showed true love for me. Yes, at times she was nice, but it wasn't genuine.

It's okay now, though. In spite of the way she treated me, I do love her now!

At first, I hated her. Yes, I said I hate it. But, the hatred was only because my love was turning sour towards people. I was tired of giving love and not receiving the love back.

I was trying to fill a void and thought that having someone to love me as a mother would fill it. However, the void was still empty. So, I was determined to fill the void somehow.

Once, we spent the night at a girl's house. I was awakened to her uncle humping on me. I was so terrified.

Thank God he didn't pull my clothes off! I think he was an alcoholic.

My screams woke everybody up. Then, the girl ordered him out of her room. After that day, I never spent the night there anymore!

Another time, I was in a trap house with some of the gang members and my friends. When I woke up, my private area was sore and some blood was in my underwear; but, my clothes didn't look like they were even taken off. So, I just shook it off, praying that I wasn't violated. I never told anybody about this either. I just wanted to block it out so I won't think about it. This is the first time I ever spoke about it.

After that incident, I decided to ask my aunt if I could come back home. Fortunately, she decided to let me come back home.

Things were going good for about a month or so. Then, unfortunately, things begin to get chaotic. I was back in school doing the same things. I was skipping classes to hang with the in-crowd.

Also, I didn't take class seriously; so, of course I just st taking classes. I didn't really care. In my mind, I was just having fun, which at the time seemed more important to me.

I also began hanging with a couple of new friends that I had met. Their sisters always had let them do whatever they wanted. I especially liked the fact that, even though she was receiving a check from the state for them, she never cheated them or took their money.

They were even given money to shop. I had been in numerous foster homes and group homes; and only one of them ever gave me more than $20 a month!

There was an older lady, possibly in her seventies, that I really liked. She was a foster parent where they placed me at. She really spoiled me! She actually let me do what I wanted. I guess since I was the youngest of the seven girls living there.

We lived out South. I attended Robeson High School, which was a lot of fun.

Boy Trouble

I hung out with a girl named Tyty, who was really cool. I used to go to her house after school. She bought me food at the restaurant as she always had money. I didn't have as much money as she did.

We both had boyfriends who were both friends: her boyfriend's name was Charlie, and my boyfriend was called PeeWee.

I had heard that Peewee had a lot of girlfriends on the side, but I never caught him. However, one of the girls and I *did* fight at school, which was really crazy.

Well, I got tired of him cheating. So, one day Charles, my friend's boyfriend, was talking to me and telling me that PeeWee shouldn't treat me like that.

Guess what: He was only talking to me like that to get me to have sex with *him*. Of course I fell for it. I was so naïve! I just wanted to be loved.

My friend found out about me and Charles, her boyfriend. I felt so bad! And, quite naturally, the guy told Peewee. So, I lost my guy *and* I lost my friend! I said that, after that day, I will never betray my friend again; *no* friend as far as that matter goes.

Later, I met this guy called *Bible* who went to my school. He was different from the guys that I usually dated. He was kind of thuggish;

more like a boss man. I could tell that he had rank. For some reason that turned me on! A lot of people obeyed him. I don't know why, but I liked that.

Bible finally noticed me, and tried to take me to his house. For some reason, I wouldn't go. I didn't want to be his play toy; I wanted him to really like me.

I would flirt with him, but I never went to his house. I guess he lost interest in me since he had other girls who didn't mind *putting out*.

Well, after that, I started calling Wood again. We started talking more often. I became homesick, so I ran away from my foster mom's house and went to my friend's Trina and Diana's house since I knew I could stay there because they were my girls! Even

if they snuck me in, at least I would be inside.

6

Trying to fill Void

We used to go on Jackson Street to this house where everyone hung out. One day we met these guys named Earl, 410, and Smokey. They were older than us, so I lied about my age.

I liked Earl's swag, and I didn't want him to think I was childish. He took me to different places, but I could tell that he knew my age; he didn't mention my age though.

Well, of course we started having sex. I was really *digging* Earl. I guess he was like a father figure to me. He yelled at me when I made him mad, but he didn't hit me. One day, he suddenly told me that he was breaking up with me. I was so crushed until I was crying.

He told me he loved me too much to hurt me; so, he was letting me go. Of course, I didn't understand.

I found out later that Earl was a pimp. I knew he had an older woman who was his age. And, he would always beat her; I just didn't know why. She hated me, and it always seemed that she wanted to fight me. Earl didn't let her fight me, though. I guess that was God protecting me. I believe God didn't allow him to make me work the streets.

I knew how the prostitute life was because my cousin was a prostitute. While growing up, I watched my cousin getting beat constantly if she didn't go out and work the streets at night. She wore wigs, short dresses and heels. I was so scared for her!

I vowed that I would never be a prostitute. But, I used to feel so sorry for her.

> *Warning: Well, I'm constantly praising God today about setting me free from Earl. God knew that I couldn't handle that life; so, he made him free me. I thank God for that!*

I also thank God for my cousin, who protected me from this guy called Cowboy, who used to hang with *her* pimp. He would often look at me, but she would tell him to leave her cousin alone.

Well, after that, I was back with Wood. I had gone back to live with Mimi, and I was doing good. I started to go back to school.

But, I later found out that I was pregnant. I was sleeping a lot and having morning sickness. One day when I was with my friends on Jackson Street, I was running and fell. I hurt my butt cheeks really badly.

Two days later at school, I was feeling very nauseous, and kept laying my head on the desk. Later on that day, I went to use the restroom and a huge blood clot came out of me into the toilet. There was a lot of blood too!

I was afraid and didn't know what was happening. I went home after that and laid down. I didn't even tell Aunt Mimi because I didn't want her to know I was pregnant. I was afraid that she would have put me out.

The only ones who knew were my two friends. I didn't know that I had miscarried; neither did I know that, after a miscarriage, the uterine walls must be scraped clean by the doctor. It was nothing but the grace of God that I didn't get an infection!

Well, I got pregnant again. Here I was, a teenage mom. I thought I would be put out of the house, so I didn't tell anyone. I wore big clothes and even a coat in the house. I later found out that my aunt had known for a long time that I was pregnant; she just didn't let me know that she knew.

Attempting to cause myself to miscarry again, I had my brother hit and kick me in the stomach. I even tried to fall off the top bunk bed onto the floor thinking that that would make me lose the baby!

When I was 6 months pregnant, I couldn't hide it anymore. I had gotten so big until I finally told Aunt Mimi and others. I had told Wood that I was pregnant, but I was told that he was telling others that he wasn't the father of my unborn child.

Boy was I stressed. I knew Wood was my baby's father. I was also stressed because I didn't want to be pregnant.

Once I went into labor, Aunt Mimi took me to the hospital. I didn't tell Wood, though, since he never said anything about the baby.

The baby didn't deliver right away either. I had to walk the hospital halls to help my baby get in position to be born. 5 hours later, my baby boy was delivered! I had 15 stitches due to his huge head.

He was so handsome and looked a lot like his dad.

Amazingly, I decided to breastfeed my newborn son. I was forced to give my baby boy my last name since my aunt threatened that I wouldn't be able to live in her house if I gave my baby his dad's last name. Since I didn't have anywhere else to go, I gave him my last name.

See, I liked the name Taiwan; so, I took away the "Ta" and added a K because I liked how K's looked – that's how I came up with his name.

I was satisfied now, though, since my baby looked like his dad. I thought that maybe he would stop cheating on me now. But, I came to understand that babies don't improve a relationship, especially if a person's heart is not in the relationship.

I went home and my aunt helped me with my baby since I had stitches and could barely walk. My stitches hurt very badly!

Great Blessing

Kye was really blessed. God blessed me to receive a lot of items for my baby at the baby shower I had. Also, since I was working, I bought a lot of baby items.

I was so anxious for Wood to see Kye! Once the time was right, I took my son to see his dad and he was happy to see him. I guess since Kye looked like Wood, he knew he was the father.

My relationship with Wood was good for a while; but, things soon got rocky between us. He was back to beating me as usual. I guess the baby didn't stop that.

A few months later, I found out that Wood had a baby with someone else. That was a shock . He didn't even care enough to let me know though. His daughter looked just like my son Kye; she was just a year older, I think.

I knew Wood was messing around with this other girl named T. But, oh was I hurt. They even went to prom. I was hurt because he never even took me to prom.

Cold Love

I noticed he would start to fight me when I came to his house without asking although it wasn't a problem before now. I could tell he liked the girl. Even though I was his first love he moved on. He found someone else who he loved.

> *Warning: So, young ladies, don't get caught up about being someone's first love. Always know that, if it is not of God, it will soon fade away. In reality, it's only lust, not love.*

I would go to Wood's house to spend time with him, but he would fight me and tell me to go back home.

One day when I came to see him, I saw white stuff on his nose. He had been upstairs with his daughter's mom. I kept wondering what that was on his face. Was that the reason he made me leave? I was really mad and confused at the same time.

Well, I had gotten tired of him; so, I was going to break up with him. I didn't see him for a long while. But, we still eventually got back together. I started going back to his house and even moved in.

Now, I was loving that I was able to live there. I was made to give all of my link to him and his mom. I didn't care since I stayed there and I didn't have any income to give them. But, after a while it wasn't good. He would fight me a lot, but not in front of his granddad. So, I used to be glad when his granddad came home!

And, I got tired of having sex all the time. I wasn't happy at all! He was constantly still going with other girls, and he would always take my link from me and any type of money that I had.

I started thinking to myself and decided to move when Wood went outside. So, this day I decided to wait till he went out late one day. I knew he was going to come in late. I just went ahead and gave him all of my link. Then, I said to myself, "I'm leaving today."

One day when he left, I already had all of Kiwaun's clothes and my clothes packed. Wood's granddad saw me leave, but he didn't tell Wood. He just turned his head as though he didn't see me.

I ran so fast down the alley, and ran into a man that I didn't know. He asked me if I was alright. I started crying and begged him if he would *please* drop me off at my godsister's house. He said yes since I had a baby with me. I was so relieved because I was afraid that Wood would beat me if he caught me.

> *Warning: Remember ladies abuse is not love! At the time, I didn't know anybody to tell. But, make sure that you tell someone if you are going through this. No woman should go through this because this abuse damages your self-esteem. I learned this the hard way.*

Hard Heart

Well, at least Lisa let me stay with her and her family. (A while back, I used to date her brother Marv.) Lisa helped me get a job at Smothers restaurant.

The job was okay; but, some customers were a little rough. One customer tried to spit on us because he felt the cook took too long. I was so mad!

Marv and I started back dating. I was kind of relieved that it didn't last long, though, because I didn't have feelings for him anymore. He had other girls too; so, I felt that he should be with those other girls.

My heart was getting hard anyway as a result of the heartaches I had already suffered.

Lisa and I would go outside after I got off work. We used to go to her baby's father's house. And, we would tamper with his car because he was cheating on her. We both would be crying about him cheating on her.

One day, she had some brown Karachi, which is brown dope. She asked me if I wanted some; so, I tried it with her. I didn't really like how it made me feel though. It kind of burned my nose too. I tried it a few more times with her, and that was it. I didn't like how my nose burned or how drowsy I was. Plus it always made me puke.

I got a little homesick; so, I asked Aunt Mimi if I could come back home. Surprisingly, she said Yes. I was so happy!

Now, I was still on the run from DCFS. I called my caseworker and asked if I could come back to my aunt's house. I hated her and I felt she hated me. When she said No, I was so angry until I cursed her out. Then, she finally gave in.

She said I wasn't responsible enough to do independent living. She really wanted me to live with other girls who had babies. But, I was tired of living in group homes and Foster homes. I wanted her to just leave me alone.

I was an angry girl who felt all alone in this world. At this time, I still was not dealing with Wood since I couldn't deal with the abuse anymore. I got tired of black eyes, busted lips, getting punched and kicked like a punching bag.

I started back hanging around Trina and Diana. We had fun hanging out all night. I paid my brother and sisters to babysit my son.

My sister Joanne was no longer at Aunt Madea's house though. She was now in a group home in Merrillville.

I met a guy named T while walking down the street. He was handsome and had dimples. He seemed really sweet.

At this time, my mom was released from jail. She started coming to our house. She was crazy; meaning, she didn't take any mess from anybody. She even wanted to fight my friend because my little brother had a crush on her. I was so mad, and my friend was terrified of my mom. My friend did not even like my brother so I don't know why my mom was tripping.

My mom even gave my Aunt a black eye! But, I don't know why.

She was living in a halfway house on Jackson and Central Park. I went to visit her sometimes. One day, I went with my mom to visit her friend. My mom introduced me to her friend, but I felt afraid of her friend for some reason; I didn't know why I was afraid at the time.

Later, I found out that my mom was trying to let this friend/lady have sex with me. Whew! I got out that jam! God allowed me to get away. He did not allow anything to happen to me.

But, that incident made me hate my mom even more! How could she set her own daughter out? But, what I didn't know then was my mom was physically and sexually abused growing up. To top that off, her foster parents raped her and made her prostitute for them. She was only fourteen at the time when that happened. Once I learned this, I concluded to myself that maybe her experiences made her think those kinds of things were normal.

> *Warning: Sad to say, sexual and physical abuse happens in a lot of homes. Unfortunately, most people just push those types of things under the rug. Regardless of whether or not it's a relative, staying overnight is not always a good idea. Make sure the environment is safe! Also, pray and get guidance from God as to whether it is ok to leave your child there. Who knows better than God!*

I really think that my mom felt that that kind of activity was normal. In fact, there was a lot of incest going on in my family. The crazy thing was that it was going on regularly, but no one was saying anything. Therefore, I have learned to pay attention to my surroundings wherever I am.

Well, I started hanging with this guy named T. I didn't know this was a setup from Satan. This guy was on drugs, but he didn't even look like it. I wasn't experienced at all; so, I guess I really couldn't tell who was or was not on drugs.

We dated for a while before I found out. We had to live with his cousin Tracy and her mom. That's when I found out he was on crack cocaine. And, he was also doing a drug called *Lean,* which is a drug made with cough syrup and other drugs.

Relieved but Scared

Wood went to jail. For me, this was a relief since he felt I could not be with anyone else although he was with other people. If I tried to be with someone else, he would try to fight me.

So, when I found out T was on crack, I left him. I went to live with my friend Tawanna. But, I found out I was pregnant! I was so mad because I knew T was the father. T would visit from time to time.

However, when I found out Wood was getting out of jail, I just left T alone completely. Mind you, by now I was two months pregnant although no one could tell.

Now, I started talking back to Wood. Wood would come over a lot; but, to tell you the truth, I didn't like him anymore. I had lost feelings for him.

He would be high off syrup, and who knows what else. And, actually I was mad that he kept coming over to our house.

I had started getting bigger; and, of course, I told him that he was the father of the baby. I was too afraid to tell him anything different.

I knew T was the father, but I didn't want a "Crackhead" to be known as my child's father. I was so ashamed. I used to give him money and even borrow money to help him with his habit. I was young and dumb. Thank God I am delivered.

> *Warning: Young ladies, never be with anyone who is on drugs. They will tell you that they are going to give up the drugs. But, if they are not ready to give up the drugs, you can't make them. Most of the time, they use the drug to cover up their pain that is down on the inside of them. It appears to help them escape the pain.*

Well, back to the labor part.

When I went into labor, I called Aunt Mimi to take me to the hospital; I went to Bethany Hospital. Aunt Mimi just dropped me off this time.

I was walking the Halls to stop the pain. I was put in a room, and I was by myself. Since I did not dilate that much, I still had time before I was ready to deliver. So, the doctor went to deliver another baby.

Two hours later, I felt like pushing. I rang the bell for someone to come where I was at. I couldn't believe that no one came to check on me.

When the nurse finally came, she saw that it was time for me to push. She called the doctors in the room, and two hours later, my daughter Kierra was born.

I love the letter K; so, of course she had to have her name begin with a K. My friend Tracy chose Latae as her middle name. She also named her Tata, short for Todd.

Wood came to see me the next day and wondered why I didn't let him know I was in labor. I didn't want him to see my baby. The nurse brought Tata into the room. Wood held her and was looking at her. I turned my head and acted as if I was going to sleep.

In my mind, I knew he was going to see that she didn't look like him. She looked like her father, T. But, I was hoping she looked more like me so that she could pass as being his baby.

When I peeked over at him, I saw he had tears in his eyes. I knew then that he knew she wasn't his. I started to feel bad; but then I thought about how he used to treat me. I decided that he deserved it!

When he left to go home, I went to sleep. Aunt Mimi picked me up the next morning to take me home. I was still living with Tawana, who was really nice.

I took Tata to Wood's house. Wood went to his mom and asked her if Tata was his child. His mom said "No." I already knew she wasn't his child though. So, I hurried up and got out of that house.

Ever since that day, we weren't really vibing anymore.

See, I was a single mother left to take care of my kids by myself. One father had stopped providing for Kiwaun after he found out Tata was not his baby. But, I didn't understand why he stopped taking care of Kiwaun since he was his child;Tata had nothing to do with Kiwaun.

So, here I am a single mom left on my own to take care of my children.

> *Warning: Young ladies, it's hard being a single mother with no help. Please stay in school and get an education. Children are expensive. You have to get pampers, milk, clothes, etc. Yes, God can help you; but, why put yourself in a spot like that? Try to stay celibate until God sends you your husband. Go to school and get a degree.*

I was still living with my friend Tawanna. I had stitches from the delivery of my baby; so, she helped take care of me while I was healing. She fed Tata to me a lot of times. She would even take her sometimes so that I could get some rest.

My friend Tracy visited me a lot too. She had met this guy though, and they were really into each other; so, I began to see less and less of her.

6 months later, Tawana was losing her place and had to move out. Since I had nowhere to go now, I moved to my sister's house that is on my dad's side.

We were getting along well! My Uncle Jerome stayed there as well. I was kind of sad there because I had to give her all of my food stamps and money. So, I really didn't have much to spend.

7

Tears

Kye got chicken pox; he was really miserable. He had a godmother who was really nice to him. She had told me that she was going to let me stay in her old apartment; but, that never happened so I guess she wasn't able to let me stay there. But, I *do* remember her saying to me "Since you are a whore, you should sell your body. I will be your Madame," she told me.

She had a house where this was going to take place. I didn't feel right about doing that, so I declined.

As I think about it now, it was not cool for her to make that offer to me. She was way older than me, and should have been encouraging me to do better instead of trying to make me a call girl.

I stopped coming around her after that.

More Changes

I met a guy named Michael, and He seemed cool. I would go to his house and spend the night.

One day when I came home, my half- sister said I had to leave her house. I was devastated! I had nowhere to go. I was very upset and scared. I took all of my things and I called my friends to help me.

Well, I moved in with Diana again. No matter what we've been through, they were always there when I needed them. They always let me stay with them when I needed somewhere to stay.

The guy I met named Michael seemed very sweet. He was handsome; and don't let me forget, he had money!

I started spending the night with him more regularly. I brought my children sometimes. At other times, my friend would babysit my children. And, kye sometimes went to his grandparents house because they always babysat him for me.

Kye's grandmother martese was always so helpful. She loved him as though he was her own child.

I continued to go to Michael's house.I saw my friend Kim during this time. She was really cool.(we became best friends). Her boyfriend was Michael's brother. Boy, was he crazy! He would hide her shoes so she could never go anywhere; not even to the store.

Anyway, I had decided to let Kye go to his grandmother's house. Marteese was his step Grandmother, but she loved Kiwuan dearly.

Wood had moved in with one of his girlfriends; so, he didn't live there anymore. I knew Kye would be well taken care of because Marteese (his grandma) didn't play about Kye. To this day, I appreciate her for that. I will never forget her kindness of keeping him whenever I needed her to.

Well, I dropped him off and went back to Michael's house. I didn't realize that Michael was just like his brother; but, I soon found that out. Yes, he would try to fight me. Oh my goodness, not again!

I didn't want to go through this again! So, I decided to leave him too when he went outside. I constantly got high off weed to get my mind off being depressed while I was over there.

After a month, I left and I didn't look back. I got tired of these crazy guys! My half-sister was saying that I kept getting crazy guys because I was crazy.

She said there's a reason I keep attracting them. So, I began to think that maybe I *was* crazy. Be careful of negative words spoken over your life. Words carry power! You will begin to believe them. Cast down any negative words spoken over you or your kid's lives. Don't come in agreement with those word curses spoken over you or your family. If it doesn't line up with the word of God don't receive it period!

Different Kind

I was looking for love, so I became very promiscuous.

I met this guy called Tank. I really liked him a lot. He was cute and had money. And, of course he was a thug. I loved the thug-type guy. We were getting along well. I was at his house constantly.

One day when I went to get my son from his grandparents' house, Kye,s father was there. He told me that I couldn't take Kye. In fact, he said I could never get him back!

I was so mad. So, I went and told my guy Tank. Tank said that I was his woman, and that we were going over there to get my son. I was a little scared but I went with him over there.

I went and grabbed Kye, and Tank made sure that no one touched me.

I couldn't believe that I finally had someone to help me and was not scared of Wood. Wood's mom was mad at me, but at the time I didn't care. I was finally free of being fearful of Wood..

More Boy Trouble

Tank took us to his house, and I was smiling for a long time. He was always a quiet boy. Tank was a good guy. He would buy me things. But unfortunately, he was a womanizer.

At first it didn't bother me; but, soon I got tired of it. So, I decided to start hanging back with Trina and Diana. I met this guy called Ty-Juan while I was at their house. I liked thuggish guys ever since Tank protected me. I was also dating other guys. I had become very promiscuous because I was looking for love.

There was a void that I was trying to fill, but couldn't for some reason. Every time that I felt like it was filled, I would still feel that I couldn't. Something was missing; I just couldn't figure out what.

Ty-Juan asked me if I would break up with Michael. I quickly said Yes. He laughed and said he was glad I did because he wanted to date me. Well, of course I started dating him. To me, he was kind of nice looking; plus, he had money.

He always got me high and drunk. I was smoking weed of course. And, he introduced me to a drink called Cisco, which was a very strange drink: I heard it had liquid crack in it.

Twisted Education

Ty-Juan kept me high and drunk; so much so until I didn't think of anything else. And, we constantly had sex all day. *That* was just crazy!

He showed me how to cook and sell drugs. He even showed me how to chop up cocaine. I was really good at it too. I would help him get his drugs together.

He spoiled me and my children. 6 months after being with Ty-Juan,I found out I was pregnant. I couldn't believe it! Of course Ty-Juan was happy though.

I decided to ask my little sister if Tata could stay with her until I get a place to stay since I wasn't really stable. My sister had agreed. But, after one week, she said that she was going to call DCFS if I didn't come and get Tata.

Of course I had no way to go and get her; my sister lived in the far South suburbs. So, I called one of my aunts. She said she could get her until I get stable. My aunt promised that I wouldn't have to worry about her trying to take her from me. Well, that definitely helped me not to be so stressed.

Later on, I found out that that was just a trick to actually get Tata from me. She got me to sign a paper while I was not paying attention, and actually not even caring at the time.

I literally signed away my rights to ownership of my child! I only signed the paper because I was told that the situation would be temporary; but, that was a lie because it was really forever.

So, my aunt in fact *did* take my daughter away from me by getting me to sign that paper. Signing that paper was a mistake that haunts me even to this day. I truly wish I had never signed that paper!

Ty-Juan and I got into an altercation because I found out he was still dating his baby's mother. So, I broke up with him. I was hurt because I really cared for him!

I started going outside with my two friends. One day, Diana gave me a laced cigarette. I took one pull, got sick and threw up. It made me feel really weird. So, they gave me some dope to try. I tried it, but I threw up after that too. It felt as if my insides were coming up as I continued to throw up. That's when I decided that that wasn't for me.

I absolutely hate to throw up, and that is all those drugs made me do! I do believe that that was God's way of making sure that I would not be addicted to those two drugs. I was pregnant anyway, and didn't need to be doing any drugs.

I met a girl named Cece. We went on a double date. She was dating Ty-Juan's friend. She was really cool. I visited her sometimes.

One day, Diana and her sisters found out they had to move. This was really stressing me out because, once again I didn't have anywhere to go.

Ty-Juan was living with his grandmother who did not like me; she liked his other baby's mother. The feeling of dislike was mutual though, because I couldn't stand her either. Ty-Juan would have to sneak me in the house; and, of course we were up to no good. She likes me now, but back then she could not stand me.

So, I'm pregnant with no place to go again. This was stressing me out; so, I decided to ask my new friend Cece. Thankfully, she said I could stay with her. That was a relief. And, since I didn't have my children with me, I wasn't so stressed.

I was messing with this guy called Cisco, too. He was very handsome, and had dimples. I had always had a crush on him from childhood. It seemed that dimples were a weakness to me.

Since Ty-Juan was away on business, I started spending the night with Cisco. That was going well until I found out that *he* was on drugs. He was tooting dope. He was so young though. How could that be? He was too cute to be on drugs. I was five years older than him. I still liked him, though.

I did notice that he was starting to have a lot of anger in him. He started having a very bad temper. Yeah, I still stuck with him though.

You're Kidding

He began to talk about me and say hateful things to me. My feelings were crushed. But, the last straw was when he had got someone else pregnant. That is when I decided to leave him for good!

I went back to Ty-Juan . He was happy to see me, too! We started going back to his house. I wanted to be with him so bad until I would even spend the night with him in a drug addict house.

The man who owned the house stayed across the street from his house. He was a crack addict. Ty-Juan paid him drugs to let us rent the room out. We stayed high and drunk.

One day, the man who owned the house we were staying in made a lady have sex with a dog for drugs!

I was in shock! I couldn't believe that drugs made her do that. And, how could he be so heartless to make her do this? I was mad and sad at the same time. I felt so sorry for this lady.

Well, Ty-Juan would leave me in the house sometimes to sell drugs. I would lock the door because I was afraid of that man. He looked really creepy. But, I got tired of being in that man's house. Since my two friends hadn't moved yet, I was still staying at their house sometimes. I was going to go to Cece's house when they finally left.

Plus, I found out that Ty-Juan was leaving me in the house sometimes just to go see his baby's mother. So, I broke up with him again and went back to my friend's house.

I either stayed in the house or hung out on the porch. One day, my friend's niece was on the porch arguing with a guy. He smacked her, and we came out to see what was going on. I snapped out on him for doing her like that. That was wrong for him to do that.

I had developed a hatred for men hitting on women since I had experienced that.

He started talking crazy, then he left. Afterwards, I found out that he was her boyfriend's brother. I still didn't know why he smacked her, but that was unacceptable.

Well, the crazy thing was I thought this guy was kind of cute, in spite of what he did.

Gotta Move

After this, Tamika made up with her brother Jerry; so, I wanted to talk to the guy that smacked her niece, whose name happened to be Dontae. We ended up talking.

He would come see me all the time, and I would go with him to his house. His mom was really nice; I loved her personality. She was really pretty too, and didn't play with her children.

Dontae was kind of crazy though. For example, one time, he came to my house and I didn't let him in. So, he went around the side of the house to the window and kept calling my name.

There was an older lady on drugs named Darlene who lived next door. When Dontae kept calling my name, her husband thought he was calling her, so they kept answering Dontae . After the third time, Dontae got mad at the husband for answering. So, Dontae told him if he answered again, he would fight him.

Well, he *did* answer again anyway. Why did he do that? Dontae went inside their house and beat up the husband *and* the lady. I was so mad! How could he do them like that?

I finally went out and made him stop. He ran out of their house and came into our house. He was actually laughing, but I didn't see anything funny at all!

I knew he was kind of crazy, though. I started going to his house; but, he soon went to jail.

8

Deeper Still

Diana and her sisters moved; so, I moved with Cece and her mom. Living there was Cece, her children, her mom, and her sisters and brothers. She became my god-sister.

She taught me how to get money from guys. I started getting my hair done regularly because my other god-sister Veah did both of our hair. She was in cosmetology school; so, she was able to keep our hair looking sharp.

You couldn't tell me anything! I thought I was too cute now. I started wearing short dresses to show off my shape because I felt like this was the way to go. I started getting attention. My stomach showed my pregnancy a little now, but I still dressed pretty.

Soon it started getting cold outside. So, Cece, her girls and I went to her house. She lived in Cabrini-Green. I used to go over there when I was younger and I lived at the group home. I used to visit people in the Vice Lord building; my friend's family stayed in that building.

Cece lived in the GD buildings. I was a little nervous at first. I'm a shy person when I first meet people; so, I started staying in the house. My belly was getting bigger; plus, I felt ugly.

Life Threatening

One day, I went to a party while I was 8 months pregnant. The party was at the end of the building where the Vice Lords hung out. Later that night some guys came and started shooting in the place where the party was. Thank God I was able to make it out!

I ran for my dear life. I ran so fast until my stomach started hurting. Boy was I grateful that I wasn't harmed! I decided that there would be no more parties for me for a while.

Two weeks later, I went into labor. My god-sister had gone with me to the hospital; and Kiwaun was still at his grandparents house. Cece left the hospital and went home.

Later that day, I had another handsome son. He was so handsome, and he looked like me.

So now I have *two* handsome sons.

Ty-Juan came to the hospital. He was so glad to see his son. He stayed up there until it was time for me to go home. He made sure I got a ride home. Then, he went to go make some money so I could get more stuff for his son

I had a lot of help. Ty-Juan didn't like coming to the projects that much; so, we talked mostly on the phone.

Emotional Times

I had waited until my 6 weeks was up; then, I went to get kye because I wanted him to see his little brother. Kye was so happy to see his little brother. Since Tata lived with my aunt, Kye never really got a chance to see what being a big brother was like. I was happy when I saw the smile on his face.

Ty-Juan had given me some money for his son. He made sure his son had everything.

Kar started getting sick when he was four months old: He kept throwing up his milk. When I took him to the hospital, they kept him. "He has something wrong with his head." they said.

The next thing I knew, his head was shaved and tools were all in his head. I was so scared! And, I didn't know how to pray.

Tt-Juan got mad when he saw him, and tried to blame me for it. But, I got mad at him too. I felt that this happened to Kye when we were smoking weed and drinking that Cisco drink, which was known as liquid crack.

Ty-Juan was crying while he was at the hospital. Every time I came to the hospital, nurses were holding Kar because everybody loved him. They said he was so handsome.

He eventually was able to come home two weeks later. I was so happy. They had him drinking milk that was very expensive. I didn't care because my baby needed to eat. But, I was able to receive WIC to get the special milk. That was a great relief!

For those who may not know what it is, WIC is a program that assists mothers with getting milk and other items for their child or children.

Sometimes it got a little hectic because Ty-Juan kept cheating with his other girls. I didn't leave him because he spoiled me and gave me whatever I wanted. I even made him buy my god-sister and me stuff.

I started doing crazy stuff. For instance, even though he would give me a large amount of money, I would hit his pockets (that means I was stealing money from him) for a couple of hundred more.

He would be drunk off alcohol and high off weed, so he didn't even know. Whenever he woke up and was looking for his money, I would act like I was innocent. I would tell him that he just gave me money so why would I steal!

Since his mom was on drugs and sometimes would take from him, I blamed her. He would believe me too. I feel bad now for doing that. At the time though I didn't care.

Once, I brought Kar to where Ty-Juan was, left him on the sidewalk in a car seat and pulled off in a car. That was just plain foolishness!

Even worse, another time I called Ty-Juan on the phone and lied saying that Karlief had fallen out the window and broke his leg. I hung up the phone, waited 3 hours later and told his uncle that Karlief had a cast on his legs and body. Boy was Ty-Juan upset. He was crying really hard. I was so dirty until I just laughed.

I felt like he should hurt since he kept hurting me. I had become evil. My heart was starting to harden.

Well, he somehow found out the truth, and got me back 2 days later. He had his uncle call me and tell me that Ty-Juan got shot. I cried really hard; I was so hurt. I did not want him to be dead. But, I found out that it was a lie, and figured out that Ty-Juan was paying me back. Boy was I mad.

His family was upset and was mad at the stupid stuff I kept doing. I didn't care though. They kept telling Ty-Juan he should leave me alone because I was crazy.

Deeper Still

The devil started taking me deeper and deeper into sin. I was selling my body for money – in the street, people call this tricking off; but, in reality I was a prostitute! Since "tricking off" is considered a fancy name, we think it is ok to do this. Actually, it is just a trick from Satan.

I had guys doing oral sex on me for money. I even learned how to hit *their* pockets. I began going out to clubs every weekend. At first, I only smoked weed; but, I started drinking too. I loved drinking because it gave me courage to say and do things I really wanted to do. And, I started calling myself Red.

Well, now Dontae got out of jail and came to where I was. That day I was on Congress Blvd. for the summer.

He saw Ty-Juan holding Karlief and went up to him and took him out of his hands. I got so scared until I went upstairs.

Dontae said that Karlief was *his* son as he took him from him. Ty-Juan was so mad at me that he was saying he was going to break my legs. Then, I called the police; so, he left. Ty-Juan stopped messing with me after that, but I didn't care. I had lost feelings for him since he kept cheating on me.

I was glad that my baby was with Dontae because I was able to be free to do what I wanted. I loved to be free to do what I wanted. I also loved going to the pool house on Congress Blvd

I had a list of numbers of guys who I was seeing. I guess I called myself a player. I mainly was tricking off or hitting pockets.

Although Dontae wanted to get back with me, I did not start back talking to him. At this time, I really wasn't into him anymore. Now that I realized I could get money, I didn't want a guy who really didn't have any.

Every night I would get on him and tell him he needs to sell drugs because I was tired of being with somebody broke. I needed a guy who had money.

One day he finally did start selling drugs to get money. But, he started going with other girls too. He even lied to his mom and said I gave him a disease, when really someone else did. At the time, we weren't even having sex; that meant he was cheating. Of course, I was mad at him. So I broke up with him.

Even though we were not together, he still took care of Kar; but, I didn't care. Now, Kar had *two* dads. I used to do that in order for my baby to have someone to fall back on whenever one dad messed up.

Yes, it was crazy! As you can see, I did so much crazy stuff.

But, of course I did eventually get back with Ty-Juan. He spoiled me a lot, so I wanted to be back with him. He was still going with a lot of girls which made me not like him like I used to.

We started going to a house on Adams. He left me there one day, and I was there for a whole 2 weeks. I was as mad as ever.

There were other guys there too. The house was a hang out; I assume it was a trap house. People did live there though.

One guy who was there was so handsome to me. He was dark-skinned, and had tight eyes and good hair. I was in love instantly, but I had to play it off. So, I was playing hard to get. He began to talk to me and we started kicking it.

I had my son Karlief with me; but, Kiwaun was at his family's house.

This guy was called Inch. He was buying food for me and my son. Since Ty-Juan never came back to check on us, I didn't care because I really was digging this guy.

We started spending time with each other while I stayed in the house. He even would play with Kar a lot. I could tell he liked children. I really liked him.

Three weeks later, Ty-Juan came back to check on us. Well, how about that! He's the one that brought me there and just dropped me off.

I told him I didn't have any food left, but he seemed as if he didn't care. He came, gave me some money, said he was doing some work and that he will be back. Of course he left me again; this time, for two more weeks. I didn't care though, because I was already digging Inch. In fact, I was glad he had left. It gave me more time to be with Inch.

He stayed at the house with me all the time. Me and the girl who lived there got cool too. She was going with one of the guys there as well.

We were always drinking and smoking weed. The mom and her boyfriend didn't seem to mind. I think they were getting paid for the people to be up there in their house.

Not Again

Inch and I started being intimate which made me like him even more. One day, Ty-Juan came to check on me. He heard that I was messing around, so he slapped me. I was mad. I yelled and talked about him real bad. He left because he said I was about to call the police.

Then, I was mad at Inch for not helping me. He did tell Ty-Juan not to hit me anymore; but, I felt that he should have hit Ty-Juan for slapping me. I wasn't talking to Inch none that day. Later though, he apologized and we were back cool. I was glad that I didn't have to hide our relationship anymore

9

Know Your Worth

Soon, I went home to get some clothes, and came right back. I eventually started spending the night at his house. Sometimes I took my children, and sometimes I left them at my friends house.

His Grandma was kind of strict; so, he would lock me in the room while he was gone. I would be in there all day while he was on the Block. I truly thought this was my king. I really had feelings for him. I even got his name tattooed on my arm! Of course he didn't tattoo my name on his arm though.

I didn't care because I loved him. He was so nice to me and my children. I felt like I finally found *the one*. But, I did end up finding out he was messing with other girls. That is when the abuse happened. He has started fighting me.

Oh my goodness not another abusive relationship! I was so in love that I felt he did it only because he was in love.

> *Warning: Never ever let anyone put their hands on you! That is not love! Love doesn't abuse anyone. See, I stayed in this relationship because I did not know who I was. When you don't know who you are or your worth, you will accept anything. I didn't know I was precious in God's eyes. I didn't know that God*

67

considered me as his princess. I didn't even know that I was royalty.

I had wanted to be around Inch so much until I joined a gang – the Black Souls. This was the second gang I was in. The first gang I was in was the Gangster Stones, which was when I was 13 years old.

Well, when Inch found out, he said he was going to beat my butt. I was scared. I still snuck into the meeting; but, eventually I ended up not going anymore. I got tired of Inch fighting me for being in a gang.

One time, Inch was fighting me and I ran upstairs. He thought I had left. All day, everyone was looking for me. Later that day, the girl Meme found me. I was on her back porch. She laughed so hard. She told me everybody was looking for me. She said Inch was going to kill me. But, I begged her not to tell me.

I stayed at her house until it was 10 p.m. She came back and said she would help me sneak out the back to go home. We quietly walked down the back stairs. When we got on the ground, Inch was under the stairs, and he jumped out. I thought I was going to have a heart attack! I could not believe he was hiding under those stairs.

Meme told him not to fight me. So, he promised her that he would not. He said he was just going to talk to me. We ended up at his house and he kept his word.

However, the fighting started back, so I ended up leaving him. Two months later, I found out I was pregnant. I would see Ty-Juan sometimes; but, ever since I lied as if he wasn't the father, he stopped treating my son nice. He didn't really do it for him anymore.

I didn't care because devontay was taking care of Kar.

I started hanging out more in Cabrini Green. There I met this guy called Skinny. We started dating and getting intimate. I really liked him until I found out he was dating all these different girls. I kept catching him; so, I started *doing me,* as they say.

I began dating quite a few others in the Greens. I was looking for love; so, I was trying to fill this void that was on the inside.

Once, I lied to this guy called Paul and told him that I was pregnant with his baby. Then, he used to spoil me and my children, so I was loving that. I would go to parties in the Greens and be so drunk until I would get put out of the party.

I could not help it though. I was looking for something, but I couldn't seem to find it.

God Heals

Well anyway, some months later I gave birth to my son who I named Keshane because Inch had told me that, if he had a son, he wanted Keshane to be his name.

After I had Keshane, I took him to see his father. At the time, he was living with his other baby's mother.

She took Keshane in and they watched him for a couple of weeks. She told me how Inch thought Keshane wasn't his because he was so skinny. I was hurt and angry. How dare he deny my son!

When I came to get Keshane, he was sick. He kept throwing up everything he was eating. I got concerned, so I took him to the hospital. It turned out that he had acid reflux.

I had to stop giving him just plain milk and start putting cereal in it so the milk would stay down in his stomach. The milk and cereal had to be really thick. The doctor said that, if he didn't outgrow it, they would have to operate on him.

I thank God that Jesus healed him. He didn't need an operation at all.

Some months later, I moved in with Inch. I was happy at first; but, later it wasn't so happy. He would fight me; so, I couldn't hang on the block that he was on. I knew the reason he didn't want me on the block was because he didn't want me to see him with his other girls he was dating.

I started back hanging with my god-sister Shay. I loved her because she was the real definition of a true friend. I never heard of her talking about me; neither did I experience her being phony. I miss her a lot.

We would hang by her house instead of being on the Block. I stole Inch's money at times to go shopping. I even started selling some of his drugs he held at the house. Since I knew how to chop the drugs, I would sell the chopped drugs to the customers who came to his house to buy drugs.

But, Inch didn't know I knew anything about selling drugs or chopping any off.

Kiwaun was always with his grandparents

Whenever I left out, I would pay his brother Terrill and his cousin Big D to babysit Keshane.

One day, Inch called saying he was about to come home to check his money because he said the amount I told him that he had didn't add up. So, I had to run back home, shay and I, to put the money back. But, I almost got caught that day.

Well, he started fighting me a lot, and I got tired of it! It seemed like he had two personalities. I later found out he was doing drugs which was why he had mood swings.

I knew he was sad a lot about his mom giving him up when he was a baby, and about his grandfather being dead. He felt as if his grandmother didn't love him like his grandfather did; but, that was not true because his grandma loved him dearly.

One day, I decided to leave, and I didn't care how he was nice sometimes. I got tired of fighting. I got tired of the girls coming to the house. I also was tired of him and his affairs with other women.

I decided to wait until he went outside. I got in a cab, and my children and I went to Cece's mom's house on Cermak. But, Inch came looking for me, and he said he was going to kill me. I didn't care. I finally felt peace from leaving him though.

I started going out to clubs with my friend Veah. She would do my hair so pretty because she was really good at doing hair. I started drinking a lot. We went out every weekend to the clubs.

I would wear colored hair…Long, red, white, and blond hair. I didn't care what kind of hair it was. We were even in hair shows a lot. I started liking to hang on the south side at the club E2 which was also called The Click.

The club was divided: one side was the Westside people, and the other side was the Southside people. I found myself going on the side where the Southside people were all the time. For some reason, I was attracted to them. They seem so much different than the Westsiders; kind of laid-back.

Once, Veah and I went with these guys from out South. The guy who liked me was mad though, because I would not sleep with him. So, he made me go into the hallway and wait for my friend.

Well, I was still thinking about Inch; he still had a part of my heart. I decided to call him devious. I had my friend call him and say that our son Keshane was in the hospital. Keshane had bad asthma; so, I used that as the reason he was in the hospital. I told her to say he was at Rush Hospital.

3 hours later, I told her to call and say that Keshane died. Inch was crying really bad. I also told her to say that she would call him about the funeral arrangements. Two weeks later, I had her call him again. This time I told her to say that the funeral was the day before, and it was really nice. But I had left a meeting with a guy, not feeling any type of remorse. She said I did not even go to the burial. She also said that she did not know why he was not invited, but she could not find his number to invite him herself. Boy was he upset.

71

He said he was going to kill me whenever he saw me. My friend and I were cracking up laughing after she hung up. At the time I didn't care because I felt I was making him sad for treating me the way he did.

Now that that was over with, I felt that I needed to find Keshane a new dad. Well, I remembered the guy called Paul who liked me. So, I went and told him that Keshane was his. Paul was happy. He started spoiling me and my children again. I felt that at least I could have my cake and eat it too.

I started going to his family's house. I still used to go out west sometimes; but, I had to hide all the time because I was scared that I would see Inch.

One time, I was with one of my friends and we had pulled up at a gas station on Congress Blvd... Inch was at the same gas station. I got scared instantly because I knew he was going to kill me. I begged her to please pull off; but, she said No. She said that I better hide. Boy was I mad at her. But, I just hid and prayed. I didn't realize how dumb it was to play that trick on him.

After my friend got her gas and her drink, she got back in the car and pulled off. I was still mad at her though. We still went to the club. Of course I got drunk so I kind of just forgot about it.

Eventually, Paul wanted me to go to his mom's house in Milwaukee. I really did not like him; but, I loved his money and how he took care of me. So, when we had to have sex, I would make him buy me some alcohol so I could be really drunk. I would also pinch Keshane to make him cry so that we would have to stop having sex.

Warning: I felt so nasty, but I loved the money though. It is crazy what people will do for money. I literally was selling my soul and body for money. But, I used alcohol to try and block out my true feelings. Alcohol seemed to block a lot of stuff. But, who all knows that when the alcohol wears off, the problems are still there. So, it's only a temporary fix.

Well, I finally agreed to go to his mom's house. When we got there, she looked at my baby's feet and said that Keshane was not her grand baby. I was shocked. How did she know?

I was so mad at her for busting my game. Well, I knew that was going to mess up my money from Paul. I started noticing after a couple of months that he started acting funny towards me. But, I didn't care.

I decided that I would go back to Inch. I had gotten tired of hiding anyway. So, one day I went on the Block that Inch hung out on, and brought Keshane. I talked to one of his friends; we will call her Mary. Mary said I was crazy when I told her the baby was really alive. He is 2 years old now.

She told me to give Keshane to her, and she would bring him to Inch. I was glad, so I left. She later told me that Inch was wondering who's baby she had. When she told him the baby was his, he cried and said he was going to kill me.

Well, Inch ended up taking Keshane in from me; he called himself kidnapping him. I called the police and the Police came on the Block; but, they said they really couldn't do anything because Inch was the dad. I was so mad.

Inch would not tell me who had my baby. Two weeks later, I found out that one of his girlfriends had Keshane. I didn't want to go get him. I believed that I was able to get my baby back. Never will I do something crazy again to my aunts.

We weren't the best of friends, but he did buy my baby things when he needed it. I knew it wasn't going to be a relationship anymore. He had his girls and I had my guys.

Yeah I was trying to fill a void so I was dating several guys. I started dating this guy from the projects. He was over the travelers. I really liked him because he was really sweet. I won't say his name, but he would come to my house a lot. We would go out to eat and go to the clubs.

Our relationship ended though because an associate lied to me. She said I said things I never said. He broke up with me which had crushed me. He didn't know that I really liked him a lot. After that, I vowed that I would stop liking anyone wholeheartedly.

I found out a month later that Inch got shot. I was so hurt. How did this happen? Later that day his friends were calling me and I was trying to figure out why. For some reason, I felt fear; but, I didn't know why!

One of the guys came. He said that he wanted to know if I had Inch's money. I didn't know what they meant. Inch and I had broken up, and weren't really talking anymore.

While the guy was outside, I called Inch's sister to tell her that, if anything happened to me, I was with this guy who was at my house. Well, me and the guy left; and I noticed that he had a gun on him. He also kept his hands on the gun.

Fear overcame me. I still don't know why I felt fear. So, I tried to talk to the guy and get him to take me to the hotel to have sex. I figured that, if we have sex, he won't try to kill me.

I kept thinking why was he not looking for Inch's killer instead of being with me. It just didn't add up. Well, I ended up having sex with him. Yes, I sold my body for Freedom.

If I only knew that God was my protector, I could have prayed. I never spoke of that day until now. I felt so low that I started to hate the guy.

The next day, I went to see Inch in Mount Sinai hospital. He was actually inside of a body bag and getting ready to go to the morgue.

The hospital employee told me that Inch died, but he will let me see him before he takes him. I cried so hard because I could not believe he was dead. How did this happen?

I kissed him on the lips and held his hand. He was so cold. He had a white band around his head where the wound was. How did this happen?

All this time I was acting so stubborn. I really loved him. I even had his name tattooed on my body. How could he leave me like this? Plus, we were on bad terms. I never got to tell him that I loved him.

I hugged him tight. I left after that and went home. I stayed in my room and cried. I begin to think about some of the good times we had.

For instance, when my children and I were with my brother. We didn't know he was in a stolen car. All of a sudden, he was speeding and trying to get away from the police. I was so scared. I thought we were going to end up in jail.

I told him about what happened and boy was he upset. But, he was glad we were ok. He could be really sweet at times, when he wasn't high.

Anyway, now I had to tell my son that his dad was dead. He was only two when his dad died; he didn't really understand what was going on though.

Now, we had to get ready for the funeral that was in a week. A couple of days before the funeral, I found out that Dontae had killed Inch. I didn't understand why he killed him.

Then, it was going around K-Town that I had set the killing up. I couldn't believe it! Why would I do that to my child's father? I was not a killer! I may have been other things, but never a killer.

I was crushed to know that I will be known as my son's father's killer. I didn't understand why this was happening. I was innocent!

Why did God let this happen? Why did God let me be framed? This was all that was running through my head.

But, I now know today that this was not God's doing; only the devil trying to ruin my reputation. He was trying to kill the promise that was in me; but, in reality he could not. Since he could not get me killed, he tried to kill me with this action.

It just seemed like everything was happening to me. Was I cursed? Did God hate me? Well, because of that incident and the lie that I was responsible, I had death threats against me.

I got jumped at a club by 6 or 7 girls. I was coming out of the club, super drunk as always. I always stayed drunk so that I couldn't really remember anything. See, once Inch died, it seemed like a piece of me had left. Even when he would beat me constantly, for some reason I loved him dearly. I loved him more than any of the guys I ever dated. I actually felt like my heart was hurting.

Anyway, when I came out of the club, I jumped. But, I was so drunk until I kind of didn't know what was going on. All I remember was some girl saying I killed their brother. I asked her who her brother was because I didn't really know. I was really wondering who her brother was.

The crazy part about this is, I was with some friends, but none of them helped me. I was so hurt. A guy broke it up and he took me home. I went into my room and just sat there crying to myself.

Now I had guys wanting to kill me. What did I do to deserve this? How did my name get involved in this? I suddenly began to hate Dontae because I felt it was his fault I was in this place in the first place. Why did he even do it?

I was living in my friend's house at that time. They saw me smiling; but, inside I was slowly dying.

Due to all of this, I didn't go to the funeral. I was afraid for my life.

Then, I found myself drinking even more. In fact, I became an alcoholic. I would drink everyday. I would drink so much until I would blackout. I was drinking so many Long Island Iced Teas, Remys, Vodkas, Parmesans, etc. You name it, I drank it.

I began to like how I felt when I was drinking. I stayed so drunk at the clubs. Also, I started going out with different guys. I was selling my body to Big drug dealers for money. I was even stealing out of their pockets when they fell asleep.

I would get pregnant, but I would go and have an abortion. I would even lie to guys that I was pregnant just to get the money to get a pretend abortion.

I will not lie. I had so many abortions until I lost count of them. To be truthful, I just wasn't myself anymore since Inch died; especially since I also was known as the one who killed him

10

Turning Point

I had started to not let anyone know who my baby's father was anymore. I hated it when someone would say they heard I set him up because I was innocent.

I even started looking into pornography, which eventually had me trying out masturbation. This became very addictive; it was hard to stop! I had just got delivered from that spirit last year. But, the devil would have me thinking it was ok since I was not actually fornicating.

Guess what? That is a lie from hell. God doesn't want us playing with our bodies. We may as well have sex! It is a set up for you all! Masturbation only opens up the door for perversion or lust to invade our minds. I'm so glad Jesus freed me from that spirit.

If any of you are dealing with this spirit, cry out to God to free you. Don't give in to the desires when they come.

We never talk about it; and many saints and youths don't know how to be free from it. Yes, I was in the church dealing with this. But, I was too ashamed to tell anyone because I felt I was the only one with this problem.

We have to learn how to tell our testimonies to help others so they can know that they also can become free! Jesus died for our freedom from any and all sin, no matter what it is!

I remember I had just left a hair show and went to the club. I used to love being in the hair shows that my hairdresser used to be in. She used to have our hair laid!

Anyway I met this guy who was at the club. I kind of liked him; only for the money though. I was already drunk, but we got even more drunk at the hotel. I guess I blacked out because I don't remember what happened after that. All I knew was that I woke up from a knock on the door. The housekeeper said she needed to clean the room.

I was shocked because the guy had left me in the hotel. He had taken my money as well. So, I was stuck way out in the suburbs, wondering how I was going to get home. I was so mad until I wanted to cry.

I was thinking to myself about how I was going to get home. I didn't have a cell phone, so I was scared. I prayed and asked God to please let me get home safely. I ended up seeing a nice truck driver. I told him my situation, and he took me home. He didn't even try anything either. That was nothing but God!

That was a lesson learned to never go with strangers anymore. I could have gotten killed. God was on my side.

Later, I saw my half-sister. She had gotten saved, and I could tell that there was a difference in her life. She stopped going out, stopped cursing, and she had a glow on her face. It seemed like she had peace too.

I can't explain it, but I wanted that too. Every time my children and I visited her, she would make us go to church.

One time I had on really short shorts and a halter top; she still made me go. One of the mothers of the church, Mother Ross, made me cover up with a t-shirt. I was so mad, but I didn't disrespect Mother Ross. I called her Mama Roz. I always respect my elders no matter what. But, I had got fed up with all of this stuff. We even went to people's houses to pray.

One time while leaving the house where the prayer meeting was, I met this guy and I liked what I saw. So, I went to his car and he called me. He was so cute. But, I didn't care about how the people from the house were looking at me.

As I think about it now, I was very bold. I know that they were praying for me though; especially Mama Roz. She was a true Prayer Warrior.

I had stopped visiting My half-sister because I was tired of going to that church. I wasn't ready to leave my life of sin. I was having too much fun; or so I thought. But God didn't give up on me. What a true father He is!

One day, My half -sister came to my friend's house looking for me. She said that God had told me to leave their house. She said God said that there was some evil in there. She said I could stay with her mom; but, I didn't think that would work. Her mom and I really didn't see eye-to-eye.

I thought to myself that I had nowhere else to go. Since I was having fun still, I would stay where I was at. I was meeting guys who were giving me money, and I was having fun at the clubs. I figured I'll pass on that.

I knew there was a God, but I really didn't know much about true salvation. So, I was back going to the clubs again, and getting really drunk as usual.

I had started selling drugs that I bought from my friend's boyfriend. One day, I had the drugs in my bosom. I took the drugs with me on a date with a guy named Charlie; I met him at the club. We went out often, and I kind of liked him.

One particular day as we were going out, we got stopped by the police. I was scared because I had an ounce of cocaine on me. But, Charlie didn't know this. I was afraid that he would kill me if he knew.

The police made us get out of the car, and they searched Charlie. Then they said they had to search me.

Boy was I scared. I prayed to myself for God to help me. Since I was a female and the officers were men, they couldn't really search me. So, the one officer just patted me down. Then, he said we could go. Boy was my heart racing!

When we pulled off, I told Charlie to take me home to go check on my children. As soon as I got there, I put those drugs under my bed. Never will I do that again.

Another time God spared me from jail was a time when my god-sister and I were selling drugs with her guy. We had the drugs in the house. The police came to our house. We started flushing drugs down the toilet. Some of the drugs didn't flush down the toilet, but they stayed afloat.

The police arrested everyone except me because they thought I was a little girl. So, I stayed in the house with the children since my children were there as well. I just thanked God for sparing me that time from jail as well! God knew I couldn't handle jail at the time.

Well, what God had told me through my half-sister finally came to light: I found out my children were being molested by someone I knew.

For some reason, I kept feeling like something was wrong. I would ask my children, but they would deny it at first. Then, one day God gave me wisdom on how to find out what was wrong. When my children finally told me, I was shocked! I couldn't believe it. I wanted to die. How could I be so dumb and not take care of my children.

I felt like it was my fault for always going out and letting them stay with others. I never would have thought someone I knew would do that to my children!

No one believed me though; But, I believed my children. Children wouldn't lie about this; plus, God had let me know it was happening. He warned me. I blamed myself for many years for this.

Finally, this year I forgave myself because it was not my fault. No matter what, I loved my children.

Well, because of the situation, I got my own place in Cabrini Green. This was my first apartment. And, due to what happened to my children, I became paranoid. I became so overprotective.

My middle son began acting out. He would kill cats, and he was so angry. As a result of this situation, I would hear voices in my head telling me to kill the boy who did this to my children. I had it all planned. But, I had to block those voices out that were in my head.

No one knew, but I had voices telling me to do evil things to people. I wouldn't listen to them though.

Later on, I started to hang out with this girl named Nene. We became really close. She had become my best friend, and we had fun together. She was really cool, and she helped me get into the Ollie store by the Greens. My children loved her dearly too.

We were like Bonnie and Clyde. That was my girl! We went to parties together, and did everything together. I also met a girl called Muffin who stayed on my ramp in the projects. She was cool as well. I considered her my sister.

My children and I kicked it with her in her place. We all started going to clubs: me, Muffin, Nene, my half-sister and Muffin's friends. We would have fun too. Oh yeah, My half-sister had stopped going to church; so, she was back hanging with us.

I started having parties at my house. I would be so drunk at parties. I would have different dudes that I was dating at the parties at the same time. Now, that's a shame!

One time, one of the guys fought me because of this. I was so drunk until I didn't feel anything. I just laughed.

Another time, the same guy gave me a black eye because I had this guy named Block in my house. But this time, I wasn't dating him. He came in with a key I had given him. He claimed he lost it though.

Anyway, I kept hearing someone banging on my door. I went to see who it was, and out of the closet came the boy called Skinny. He smacked me in my face. He was very tall. Block and my children came into the room where we were. My oldest son had a knife.

Block didn't even defend me. He went out in the hallway to talk to Skinny. Boy was I mad; so, I locked my door and made Block stay out there in the hallway. I kicked him out and didn't let him back in. I couldn't have no guy around me not defending me.

After that, I lost respect for Block. I stopped liking him like I used to.

I've been with so many guys until it's a shame. I had not had sex with all of them, but I just couldn't seem to fill my empty void.

I had just met this guy called Donald. I kind of liked him, but not really. He took care of my boys and me. He ended up moving in with me. I still saw other guys though. This time, I met the other guys down at my sister Muffin's house.

Donald stopped making money because he couldn't get any more drugs. So, of course I didn't want to be bothered with him. He started to irritate me now that he was broke. I even put shrimp in his mouth when he was asleep. See, he was allergic to shrimp, and it made him swell up. That was really dirty of me. How could I do that?

His cousin started going to Iowa to sell drugs. They were about to go again on this particular day. I told him that he had better go with his cousin because we needed money.

A group of us had moved to Indiana and we all stayed in this one house. So, we needed money to pay bills, and my boys and I needed clothes. He didn't want to go, but I was going to make him. Yet, for some reason he did not go.

The next day, his cousin and his friend ended up getting killed. I couldn't believe it! They were driving and drove off a cliff, thinking it was an exit. It was so sad. Everyone took their deaths hard. And see, Donald would have died with them! See how we never know when our last time is?

When we moved from Indiana, I moved back to my apartment in the Greens. Ofcourse I didn't want to be bothered with Donald; so, I put him out so he can date someone else.

11

The Last Straw

My friend had moved to Minnesota, so I was by myself now. Nene and I were cool, but not as we used to be. We stopped hanging out a lot. We actually ended up getting into a fight. And, I was hurt because I really didn't want to fight her.

Well, after the fight when I came to the building, there was a group of people who were about to jump me. They had guns and weapons. I was scared because I heard a voice say that I was about to die. I told God to please not let me die; I knew I was going to hell if I did die. I didn't want to burn for eternity. I told God if he didn't let me die, I'll get saved.

Suddenly, the building manager came to stop the fight. I was escorted to my place. I then took some stuff to my sister's house. I was hurt because I had called family members to help me, but no one came. They said No.

So, my children and I stayed at my sister's house. I had met a praying woman named Earlene. I made her my godmother. I would go to her house often. She was really close to God.

I often asked her to pray for me to get a job, car, and a place to stay. Every time I went to her house, she would tell me that I needed to be saved. But, I wasn't ready yet, even though I told God I would get saved. But, because of her prayers, God started dealing with me.

At home, I started listening to gospel music. I was an alcoholic as well. But, one day, I didn't have the desire to drink anymore. I pulled out the drinks that I had in my fridge and poured it out. God delivered me from alcohol that very day just like that.

No, I didn't even have to go to A.A. God was my A.A! God also blessed me with a job at Rush Hospital starting off with $13.50 an hour. I was so glad.

See, I know God did it because everyone had to show their diploma except me. The man didn't even ask me for my diploma. I know God did this because I didn't have a diploma then. I never told anyone about it either.

That pushed me to get my diploma though. So, later on I receive my diploma! Well, I still was going to the clubs and kicking it with guys; but, I eventually became tired. I was tired of my life and I knew there had to be more than just this.

I had already tried to commit suicide when I was at my friend's house. I went to stay at her house for a while. I wasn't really happy though. I got tired of living from place to place. I was tired of going with guys and going to the club's! I was tired of this life.

So, I started going to church. The church bus would pick me up. There was a lady named Irene whom I will never forget! She gave me a card and a gift card that touched my heart. I still have the card to this day!

Unfortunately, I got pregnant again; but, of course I got an abortion. I just couldn't take being pregnant anymore. It was already hard being a single mom.

Well, I didn't really understand about being saved. I thought that just going to church meant I was saved. After church, I still kicked it with guys, had sex with them and went to the clubs.

One day, I was just tired of my life. I was thinking about killing my children and myself because I didn't want them out here suffering without me. No one would take care of them like I would. No one will show them love like I would.

For some reason though, I ended up calling the pastor to talk to him. I called and left a message; but, the pastor never returned my call. I was so hurt. I didn't want to go there anymore. I felt that the leader wasn't there when I really needed him.

My sister had given me contact info of a pastor she knew; so, I called him to get a ride to church. He came to pick up my son and me. But, instead of him trying to talk to me about my problems I was going through and how to seek God, he had tried to make advances at me. I was very mad about that.

Here I am hurt and trying to find God, and here he is trying to make advances. I know I wasn't saved, but I did know that it was wrong to cheat on his wife; and he was a pastor.

I will never date a man of God, let alone a married man. I never messed with married men. I may have done wrong, but that was one thing that I said I would never do because one day I might want to get married. So, that was something that I didn't agree with.

So, my heart began to harden. I felt like I was in need of spiritual help, but I just couldn't find it.

Well, my sister took me to this other Church, but they were acting funny. They thought that we only came to eat, and were saying things like they didn't have any food.

They also were saying they hoped we weren't trying to come to eat. But, I wasn't hungry, I had money to buy food if I was hungry. I was looking for spiritual food!

So, now I got fed up with church. I said that I will no longer go back to church after this happened. I kept going to Earlene though. She was so nice to me. She always smiled and never complained. She was going through a lot, yet she didn't complain.

She had a relationship with God that was so close until they even laughed together. I never knew that God laughed before then. I always was told he was someone who was always mad at us.

Every time I came to Earlene's house though, she kept saying God wants me to be saved. I would tell her that I wasn't ready though; I would ask her to just pray for me to get a house and a car. How selfish I used to be.

But yet, God still loved me in spite of that. One time, she told me that God was warning me that someone was going to try to rape me. She said that God said don't ever get on the elevator by myself in Cabrini-Green. That scared me so bad.

After that, whenever I was in the projects and I got on the elevator, I would hurry up and get off whenever someone got on. I didn't know who it could have been though.

I used to dress half-naked, feeling like I had to show my body to get attention. I thank God for sparing my life and warning me. He didn't have to, but he did.

Earlene was still saying I needed to be saved, but I would tell her that I'm saved. I told her that God didn't tell her the whole revelation. In my eyes, I was saved. I didn't know that I had to stop sinning. I thought I could still drink and go to clubs as long as I went to church.

God wanted me to change my ways. I would soon find out how.

Well, my sister told me she had one more church to check out. So, I told her I will; but, after this I was done with churches. Well, I called the pastor and asked to be picked up from work. I told my boss I was going to work through my lunch so I could get off early. She said okay.

At 1:00pm, my boss came and asked where my friends were. I told her I didn't know. This time I told the truth. Usually, me and my friends would go hide for hours after we finished working. This time I didn't go with them.

I just wasn't myself lately. I was looking for some peace, and I really didn't know how to find it.

Well, since I didn't tell my boss my friends' whereabouts, she said I couldn't leave early. I was so mad. I told her "Fine! I don't need to go to church anyway!" And I hung up on her. But, she called me back and told me to go to church and leave early. She said that I needed to be in somebody's church.

So, Brother Dixon from the church came and got me. Boy could he talk. We talked the whole ride. When I got to the church, I had my guards up though. I have been through so much, and I was just tired of being tired.

At the church, Sister Taylor was so sweet. She walked up to me and asked if I wanted to sit up front with her. I yelled at her with a mean voice saying "Do it look like I want to go up there!" She looked shocked and just said okay.

I feel bad now because she is one of the sweetest persons I know! She is also my baby's godparent.

Anyway, I sat down and listened to the pastor. The Elder came where I was and asked me to go to the back, turn around, just focus on Jesus and say

Thank You. I did what he said, and tears began to fall down my cheeks. It feels like some type of peace suddenly fell upon me. It was a feeling I never felt before.

I was so glad I came. After that, I started coming more often. I still was smoking weed, going to clubs and having sex. But yet, I still felt drawn to come to church more.

12

Transformation

My boss at my job said she noticed a change in me. I also stayed to myself more. I started reading my Bible and praying more. I didn't want to do what I used to do at work.

I found myself doing my work now and not playing around, which was a big difference in how I used to be. I would come to work so drunk after leaving a club. I would punch in and go home to sleep; then pay someone to have them do my rooms.

I would also come to work, find an empty room and just go to sleep in the room until my shift was over. I used to curse like a sailor. Every word I said was curse words. I was a hot mess; I admit it!

Then, one day when I went to Earlene's house, she told me that God was about to save me. She read a scripture out of Revelation and I got scared. She told me that it wouldn't be long.

A week after that, I had a dream that the end had come and I was left behind. I didn't understand why I was left behind. I kept saying in my dream that I was saved; why was I left behind. God was letting me know that my heart wasn't right.

After that dream God showed me that I had to give all of that up in order to be right with him.

I know people always say that God knows their heart; and, Yes He does. And, yes, our hearts can deceive us. We have to ask God to change our heart! Jeremiah the 17th chapter and the 9th verse says "The heart is deceitful above all things, and desperately wicked. Who knows?"

Well I finally surrendered to God! I was praying and asking God to bless me with my own place. I was living with a relative at the time. We were really going through. I would cry every day in my room, and read my Bible. The relatives would lock my children and me outside in the cold. It would be below zero, and we would be freezing while waiting for them to come home. I didn't understand why God was allowing this to happen.

I started calling this subsidized site. Each time I called, they said they had no vacancies. I had already been into many folks' homes, and I was being treated very badly. The more I was suffering, the more I prayed and read my Bible.

One day, my pastor told me that God was about to bless me with my own place. Two weeks later, the housing man called me. He told me to come to the office. I came, and he showed me a list that had 250 people on the list. He said he was going to put me on the list like I was already on there; and, he put me on the top.

That was nothing but God who did that! I was so happy until I cried. I finally had my own place! I went to my relatives' house and grabbed my children.

I called my son's Uncle Tyrone and asked him to buy me some food, a pillow, and a comforter. He took us and bought all of those things. When he dropped us off, I was so happy. We slept on the floor, but I didn't care. I finally had my own. I was so grateful for my place. I finally had peace.

Living with others is an experience. I do appreciate those who let me stay with them. It also helped me become closer to God. So, no I'm not mad at what I had to endure from living with them.

Sister Taylor gave me a book called *No More Sheets* by Juanita Bynum. When I read it, God started dealing with me. I would call Sister Taylor to see if this was God. I asked her if I was supposed to give up everything that I got and that I bought for myself. She told me that, if that was what God was telling me, then I needed to obey. I'm laughing to myself now because I was just being stubborn.

Well, I decided to obey God. I gave away everything the guys gave me. I tried not to give away the TV, but someone ended up stealing it from me. I couldn't even get mad about them stealing it because I knew that God wanted me to give it away.

So, I ended up moving into my new place with nothing; I didn't even have a TV. We played games, prayed and read the Bible. I had gotten so close to God! Nothing took my time from God. I was so excited by what God was doing.

Later, someone who was my neighbor offered me a TV. Ofcourse I took it because I felt my children needed it.

While I was reading my word I heard God tell me to give it back. I was confused. I know God wasn't saying to give it back? I told God that my children need a TV. He told me again to give it back.

God asked me if I trust him, and I said Yes. He told me again to give it back since I trust Him. So, I went and told my neighbor that I had to give the TV back. He asked why? I told him that God said give it back! He started laughing and said to tell God what's up.

He came and got the TV, and then started talking bad about me to others. He said I was crazy, claiming to talk to God. I didn't care though because I really wanted to please God.

I had got to the point that I did whatever God told me to do. My heart's desire was to please God. As a result of this, I started getting checks out of nowhere! I even got unexpected checks from my job; and I was the only one who was getting checks.

Now these were *big* checks, not little ones. I started going to the park with my children. While they were playing, I was reading the Bible by the pond and passing out tracks. I was so happy to be saved!

God started using me at my job. I became afraid, though, because people were saying that God doesn't use us at work. So, whenever the Spirit of God came upon me, I started trying to stop it; but, I couldn't. Once the Holy Ghost comes upon you, you *will* obey God!

Well, he had me praying for some of the patients, and just their beds when they were gone. How I knew it was God leading me to pray like this was by the fact that, whenever He had me praying, the doctors would be at the door but they never came in until I finished.

Someone even reported me to the hospital manager. I was so scared when he called me to meet with him. He didn't fire me; he only told me to try not to pray at work.

I started getting even closer to God and bringing more souls to Christ. No work of my own, but all the glory is given to God. Yes, I was going through, but my faith in God had me trusting Him.

I still kind of wanted to tip and date. It was a void still on the inside that wasn't closed.

One time, I met this big-time drug dealer. He had a nice car; the type of guy I liked. This guy was a nice package from Satan. Well, I fell for the Trap; even had sex with him. Afterwards, I felt so guilty until I told my best friend.

Well, I was sneaking and seeing him. Then, one day my friend Aleta called me to tell me what God said: He was going to turn His back on me if I kept sleeping with that guy.

I was afraid. I didn't want God to leave me. So, the next day I told the guy I had to stop seeing him. He became really angry and said that it wasn't over until he said it was over. I got scared and just started saying Hallelujah on the phone over and over until the Holy Spirit started to take over.

I started speaking in tongues. Tongues is a Heavenly language from God. When I finished, he hung up the phone.

He told me that he told his friends what happened; and they said I was pretty but nuts! Well, after I stopped answering his calls, he eventually gave up! Boy was I glad.

After that, I started praying more and reading my word. Antoinette and I had started going to people's houses praying for them and telling them about God. People called us Batman and Robin. We both had a heart for Souls.

We didn't care if it was cold outside; we were going out to reach the souls. Of course, when you are doing God's will the devil will come to attack you.

One day while I was at work, this lady from my job wanted someone to take her to the grocery store. I volunteered because she was such a sweet old lady; or, so I thought.

Well, at the time, I was staying at my friend's house because my lights were off. But, I didn't tell her where I was going. That Saturday, I went to pick up the lady.

When I got there, she gave me a *big* cup of tea; I mean, it was huge! I heard someone say pour it out. I waited until she went to the back, and I poured It in the sink. When she came back to where I was, she wanted me to drink some more. I told her No because that was a huge cup already.

We left out and went to the store. Instead of her buying food for herself, she was trying to get ingredients to get cookies for my church. I was surprised! I thought to myself, "Why would she lie and say she needed to go to the grocery store?"

I told her that my pastor doesn't eat from everybody, and it will be a waste to get stuff to make cookies. So, she only grabbed a couple of items. So, I'm now wondering what was going on.

When we got back to our house, she kept trying to give me valuable items. I kept declining, but I finally gave in and took a vase. The vase was worth a lot of money.

I put it in my trunk and went back to Antoinette's house. I sat down to watch TV. About 30 minutes later, she got up and went into the room and prayed. It didn't seem odd because she always prayed.

Well, she came out of her room a few minutes later and said God said I went somewhere I should not have. She described *everything*. I knew it was God because I had not told anyone where I went. She said that God said a spirit was attached to my back from touching the vase. The lady had attached a demon to the vase. It turned out that the lady was a witch.

I started crying. I called my pastor in a panic. He didn't know what to do; so, I hung up and called one of the sisters in Christ. She talked to me, and prayed and told me to pray until the spirit on my back left.

So, I went to the bathroom and cried out to God. I prayed so long until I fell asleep in the bathroom. I had a dream later, though, that Jesus had hugged me and said it was well. I was so glad that it was over!

I never went anywhere else without asking God first! And, oh yeah I got rid of that vase!

> *Warning: That same lady used to cook for people at my job. She always brought food everyday to people at the Rush Hospital. That is why you should not eat from everybody. You don't know whether these people pray evil over their food. Always pray over your food and let God lead you before you eat at people's houses.*

Of course the devil was mad at me. I was constantly, by the grace of God, bringing souls to God. I really just didn't want anyone to be lost.

Sometime after that, though, I received a letter asking I wanted to join the Illuminati (a secret society). I didn't know what that was at the time. It was a typed letter that said someone from the Block referred to me; and the letter said I had lots of gifts on the inside of me that could be used.

The letter went on to say that I could be rich, and have someone fall in love with me; or, I could kill my enemies. It also said a lot of famous people were in Illuminati.

I was told in the letter that, if I wanted to accept the offer, I should send the letter back to a PO Box that was in the letter. The letter stated that I would not know who was in

Illuminati or who sent the letter to me until I accepted the offer.

It also said that, after I accept the offer, I will be picked up and blindfolded until we reach the destination, where I will be initiated into this secret society. After that, I started getting magazines that had demonic weapons and robes that people from cults wore. I became scared but didn't know who to tell. I didn't want to be called crazy; so, I just threw the books away and started praying.

Later, one of the neighbors brought me to her house and told me that I could have my house like hers, and I could get a brand new car for $600; or, my children could get a paid scholarship for whatever College they wanted to go to.

She told me that she could help me with anything I needed. I don't know why she told me this. I actually figured that she may have been one of the people who referred me to the Illuminati. Matter of fact the letter said there were quite a few people on my block that were in the Illuminati.

Well, one of the church members needed a place to stay. I was asked by church members to let her stay, so I did. One day, I was praying because prayer was my life; I always prayed. This particular day while I was praying, the girl started crawling like a snake. I was scared.

I stopped praying and began pulling her towards the door and halfway out the door; she finally came to herself. I was so scared after that. This incident made me not pray anymore while she was at my house, because I didn't want her to manifest again.

A month later, the man next door was sitting on the porch. He looked so weird to me; there was just something about him. One day, I was home and I asked him if he was a warlock. He said Yes. He asked how I knew. I told him that I didn't know. But, God told me.

I asked him why he served Satan. He said that he was molested at a young age, his mother used to get beat by his stepdad, and he used to beat both his mother and him. So, he felt that, if there *was* a God, why would he allow all of that to happen.

I told him Jesus loves him and Satan is the one that allows that to happen. He said Satan gave him powers; and I said Jesus is more powerful than Satan. Then, he got mad and said he would kill me if he wanted to. I told him that he can't do anything that God won't allow him to do. I gave him a book about it which we got saved, and he took it and went in the house.

13

No Other Option

The girl from my church stayed with me for 4 more months. While she was at my house, I didn't really pray that much; afraid that that snake spirit would manifest again.

I noticed I begin to slowly get weak spiritually. Therefore, my flesh started coming back. So, I started back talking to this guy I knew before. He was a nice guy. He started telling me everything I wanted to hear. I also wanted him to be my husband. I started liking him a lot!

During this time, I also started going to this Hospitality program at McCormick Place. After me and Fl started messing around for a minute, I got so convicted; so, I stopped seeing him.

But, the devil had already pulled out my old stronghold which was lust. Lust is very powerful! I think I would have stayed with him, but I knew he really didn't want to be saved. I knew I had to let him go and stop trying to put together something God didn't put together.

It's just like a puzzle. No matter how long or how much you try to force your own piece of puzzle in the wrong place, it just won't fit If it's not meant to be in that spot. It's the same way with a relationship. If God didn't place the person in your life, they won't fit; no matter what you do to try to force it to fit.

A couple of months later, I took Keshane to get his haircut and ran into this guy named Marcus. I knew him from when I used to hang out with Keshane's dad.

Marcus used to seem so nice when I was going through with Inch's death. Well, at the time I was driving the church's bus, and I was still the Pastor's nurse. Mind you, I was hardly feeding my spirit man anymore.

Anyway, we both exchanged numbers. He claimed he wanted to see Keshane. I would pick him up, and then we would just be talking and kicking it. I found myself calling him a lot.

Well, one day when he came, we had sex. He still seemed nice though. He would help me with things when I needed help. He had a girlfriend, but I didn't think anything of it since we weren't really involved.

God wasn't pleased with me. It even seemed like I felt His Spirit leave me. I felt so guilty until I stepped down from my position at church. I also was about to be ordained as an evangelist. But, how could I be a pastor's nurse or evangelist when I was constantly fornicating?

I knew that was wrong. My pastors were disappointed with me; but, I seemed to be in a trap that I couldn't get out of. To tell the truth, at the time I didn't want to get out of it either.

I was still attending the hospitality program. I got hired at McCormick Place as a receptionist. 2 days later, the lady who hired me told me that she was told not to hire me since I came to class late one day. I was in awe. But, I knew that God had allowed this to happen.

A week later, I got hired at Gateway as a youth counselor. The next day after I was hired, I received a call to say that they could not hire me. The reason was because they had enough ladies; so, they wanted a man. They told me that they would call me back when they had another position open because they really liked me.

God showed me through this that only he can open doors, and he also can close the doors. I was hurt; but, instead of repenting and getting back close to God, I kept on sinning willfully.

> *Warning: I told myself that I would bring Marcus to God. How many know that that thought was a setup from Satan? Either you will bring them in or they will bring you out. Well, guess what? He brought me out!*

It started so slowly though. One minute I was listening to secular music instead of gospel. Then, I started cursing again. I started letting my boys hang out with their friends and family. I even found myself drinking again.

I found out a couple months later that I was pregnant. I didn't want to be pregnant. Well, I told God that I wanted to marry him then. As soon as I said that, Marcus changed instantly. The cover came off!

He was no longer that nice Marcus I knew. He started hitting on me. He would accuse me of having sex with my children, and my brother, and even with his mother; with his sisters, and his uncles. I was in such awe! How can he think such crazy things?

I started drinking more with him. I started being emotionally abused by him as well. The crazy part was that I was still going back to him after all of that.

As a result of this treatment, I didn't want to keep the baby I was now pregnant with. So, I had an abortion to get rid of my baby. The crazy part was, earlier that day, my friend Aleta called me and asked if I was trying to abort my baby. How did she know? She was all the way in Indiana; and I didn't tell anyone except Marcus's sister and Mom, and she didn't know them. I was now living in Chicago. Plus she didn't know anyone I hung out with.

She said that God said don't get rid of my baby. I listened to what she said, but it went in one ear and out the other. Well, of course I still had the abortion anyway.

After the abortion, I started feeling a lot of pain in my side. I also had heavy bleeding; so, I went to the hospital. I told them what I did. They gave me an ultrasound and told me that the sack was holding on!

I cried and I was so mad at God. "How could you protect my baby from harm?"

Well, they kept me overnight, then I went home the next day. They wanted to make sure I was okay. When I got home later that night, Aleta called me again. She laughed

and asked if I did it anyway. I cried and said Yes. She said God said the baby wasn't going anywhere; and that he was going to use my baby at a young age. He also said I would never be in need of my baby; He will meet my baby's needs. A lot of people won't like her because of the calling upon her life.

I became so depressed. I told my church I was pregnant. A lot of people were disappointed. I felt so bad! How was it that I was just bringing in souls to Christ, praying for them, and was just about to be ordained as an evangelist by my pastor; now, I'm here pregnant and not even married.

The hurting part was that a lot of people from the churches started treating me very differently. Those who always hugged or greeted me turned cold towards me. Some didn't even speak anymore. I was so hurt and wanted to die. Little did they know I hated myself for what I had done.

I had a best friend who also kind of distanced herself from me. Even though I smiled, I was so torn on the inside. The low self-esteem I had growing up had resurfaced.

Eventually, I stopped going to church. But, what really encouraged me was how Mother Collins and Sister Aleta came to see me. They drove all the way from Indiana to pray for me and encourage me! That meant a lot because they came at a time when I wanted to give up so bad.

When I was 8 months old, I went back to church. It took a lot for me to hold my head up while I was pregnant. I felt like I let God down so bad. I felt stared at me; but yet I would hold my head up.

No one knew that inside I was dying. My baby had become breech. So, my pastors had prayed and laid hands on my belly. The next day I felt my baby turn around. It hurt really bad when she turned. But, I was glad that my baby turned so that I wouldn't have to have a C-section.

I was sick during the whole pregnancy. A lot of foods made me throw up; and I was always nauseous. During all of that, I went to school and got all A's in my classes.

My due date was December 14th, but I had my beautiful daughter on Christmas, December 25th. I was in labor for 2 days. She just didn't want to come out.

I had stopped talking to her dad because I didn't want to be stressed while I was pregnant. I didn't tell him where I had delivered my baby either. I didn't want to be around him because all he did was argue and talk negatively about me; so, I just stayed away.

Since I didn't know my true identity, I didn't really start to come back around him until I had Kayla. I brought his baby to see him. He was nice at first, but the real him came out eventually. He was seeing other girls; but, yet I kept holding on.

I didn't know my true identity: Royalty and A King's child which meant I was an heir. Low self-esteem didn't let me recognize that though.

I began to eat a lot of food because food became my comfort. I gained a lot of weight. Every time I would be mad or sad or angry, I would eat because food just seemed to soothe me.

I didn't realize that I could come to God instead of making food my God. That's what I did when I chose food over God: I made food my god.

14

New Beginning

I begin to drink and smoke weed. I started dating other guys, thinking that will get Marcus's attention. It did get his attention for a little while; but he was still the same.

God constantly reached out to me. He was calling me back to Him, but I ignored it. Hey, I got to the point that I got tired of being cheated on; tired of the physical and emotional abuse. I was tired of him doing what he wanted, but coming to my house to eat, sleep, and wanting sex.

Now, I was ready to leave, but God let me stay for a minute. I believe God let me stay so that I would see that this time, once I leave or he lets me go, I won't ever go back.

I left my church because I felt dead on the inside. I needed help to be free from fornication, low self-esteem, etc.

I began visiting New Vision Of Victory International Ministries. Each time I came, I felt the love that I needed. I was so broken up on the inside until I didn't want to feel the pain I felt anymore on the inside.

I felt like a failure as a mother. My two youngest sons were on drugs and drinking, they both joined a gang and they were also going in and out of jail. I didn't have a relationship with my oldest daughter. Since she lived with my aunt, they created division between us. My oldest son wasn't communicating with us anymore. I lost my good-paying job. Nothing seemed to be going right anymore.

On Sundays, I made myself go to church. I would just have left out of the bed with my daughter's father; I couldn't get rid of him. This time, he wouldn't leave. I had started hating him.

For some reason, he kept coming to my house. I even stopped tripping when he would talk to other girls on the phone. I didn't care anymore what he did. I didn't check his phone anymore. I would be so mad when he came to my house at night. I even began to hate when we had sex; my mind wasn't in it anymore.

I felt like the prodigal son who lost everything - material things, spiritual things, my children, my self-esteem, my confidence, my job, my finances, etc. My house even got robbed of everything! I had a 55-inch TV, 2 40-inch TVs, one 32-inch TV computer, jewelry, game systems, clothes, food, etc. I was down to nothing like the prodigal son.

But, like the prodigal son, I came to my right mind. I remembered my true identity! I remembered my Father God was a King! So, I didn't have to settle for less! I didn't have to eat from the pig's bin anymore since my Daddy (God) owned the whole world! So, I decided to go back to my father's house. I didn't care anymore about not being used by God. I just wanted him to love me again, and to take my pain away.

God took me back with open arms! He didn't judge me like others did. He led me to my spiritual parents who truly loved me. They didn't judge me at all! They gave me the love that was needed as parents. I never experienced love from my parents. They also never gave up on me. He also gave me my Coach Sophia who has really helped me go after my purpose. I also think God for my CCl & CBK family! They helped me as well, alone with different ones God placed in my path! You see God let me know my tears have a purpose. It has a story that was needed to help others.

So you see, my tears were not in vain. Even though then I didn't understand why I had so many tears but now I understand. My tears were made so God can get the glory out of my life. And just like he captured my tears he will put yours in a bottle as well because your tears have a story as well! You have a purpose! Never ever forget that!

Well, as of today, I am now free from bondage! Praise God! The stronghold that was between me and my daughter's father is broken. Also, I graduated from Bill Winston Ministry School, and I am now enrolled in real estate school to receive my real estate license, and want to start a mentor program for youths.

I am now reaching out to others to let them know they can make it, regardless of what all the devil throws at them in life. And, In spite of how many times you messed up! Just know that you have a father who loves you dearly. He is waiting with open arms like He was for me.Your tears were not in vain. Your tears have a story just like mine did. Jesus has your tears in a bottle waiting for you to tell that story so you can help free someone else who may be bound.

Just like *this* prodigal daughter was able to come back, so can you! Trials may come, children may even be out of control, bills due, etc. Just remember your Father God loves you dearly! Your tears have a story! I am now driven to become a motivational speaker to reach out to those in prisons, juvenile detentions, group homes, shelters, schools, and wherever else I may be needed to let others know that they too can make it just like me. Your father God has an expected end for you!So, here I am, a new person in God. God has given me my signet-ring, a robe, and a feast! I pray that my story helps you to know that, no matter where life takes you, and how many tears you may shed. You still have PURPOSE! Remember, God is married to the backsliders! There is life after death!If God can change me and forgive me, He can do it for you!

Be blessed!

MY TEARS
—Have A Story—

Darlene Williams shares her true life experiences that led her away from the Lord and took her into promiscuity, self-hatred, abuse, etc.

Darlene keeps it as real as she can to let others know that no matter what your situation is there is still purpose in your tears! Because your tears have a story.

Ihaveavoice1@yahoo.com
TikTok: @1ihaveavoice
Instagram: *darlene_bloodline-breaker*

www.ingramcontent.com/pod-product-compliance
Lightning Source LLC
Chambersburg PA
CBHW071231090426
42736CB00014B/3041